What You Might Have Missed

Volume 1

What You Might Have Missed

Volume 1

Owen Watson, Ph.D.

TURN THE PAGE
IN YOUR LIFE

What You Might Have Missed
Volume 1

First Edition

Cover Design By: Owen Watson, Ph.D.

Editor: Ramona L. Watson, Ph.D.

Library of Congress Cataloging-in-Publication Data

ISBN-978-1-957420-10-3

Contents

PREFACE

I will be the first to tell you that I am not (and am far from ever being) the "know-it-all" for interpreting Biblical scriptures, but I am someone who believes in and enjoys a lifestyle of spending personal time with God by fasting, praying, reading, discussing, researching, and learning His word. There is nothing about me that's special and qualifies me any more or less than anyone else. However, I find great peace and delight in knowing God (as the triune Godhead – Father, Son, & Holy Spirit), His ways, and greatly benefitting from His love and mercies toward me.

Having God integrated into my everyday life has ignited a passion within to share revelatory impressions of His scriptures (interpreted, supported, and referenced by Bible verses) with others. As with all believers who are loyal and committed to walking with God, there's a responsibility for each of us to gradually expand His kingdom here on earth by "being about our Father's business" with the gifts and talents He has bestowed upon each of us. One of God's gifts I've been given is interpreting and declaring scriptural messages, which is conveyed through my talent and love for Christian faith-based writing. It allows me to glorify God and bless others by producing and presenting relatable, simplified Christian books for nurturing spiritual growth and relationships with God among believers.

INTRODUCTION

With so much vying for our attention, causing us to juggle priorities and goals for each day, it is very easy to miss the small but significant aspects along life's journey. Just think about it for a moment. For instance, how many times have you found yourself departing your house (on a route you've traveled maybe hundreds of times) with a laser-focused mind on getting to where you're going and doing what you must do, but failing to remember what you've passed along the way once you've arrived? Once your goal has been achieved and you're returning home, you seemingly noticed something different along the route as you "duhishly" think and say to yourself (maybe something like), "When did they post those speed signs?" By then, the blue lights are flashing behind you followed by a loud, abrupt siren signaling for you to pull over - lol. Truth is, the "significant" speed signs have been there all along, but you were so focused on your goal that it distracted you from the obvious markers along the way.

Much like that example, many of us who read the Bible do so either by taking it at face value, maybe as a goal to hastily read it in a year, or as a way of learning about and/or communicating with God (whether daily or whenever the "urge" arrives) etc. Whatever the reason or amount of time spent, the result remains the same for everyone who reads or studies the Bible, and that is because of our focus, some things will be missed. Here's a good kicker: no matter how many times any of us read, study, or even preach or teach the entire Bible, there are always newly discovered nuggets which oftentimes relate to either something we're facing, someone else around us is facing, the state of our nation and/or the world, or maybe something enlightening that piqued our interest unlike previous times when we read certain passages.

In *What You Might Have Missed (Volume 1)*, we will trek through the Old and New Testament books of the Bible consisting of Genesis (chapters 1 through 11) and Revelation (chapters 1 through 11). Throughout each chapter there will be a focus and discovery regarding key scriptures which many may have read but not given much thought to (i.e., Why was Eve's penalty for sin centered on married women and women who were able to bear children (Genesis 3:16)? What is the significance of God limiting the days of mankind to 120 years (Genesis 6:3)? How will everyone be able to see Jesus coming with the clouds (Revelation 1:7)? Who are the 144,000 (Revelation 7:3-8)? etc.). There are numerous scriptures which have or will intrigue many new and seasoned believers alike; however, the intent of this book is to promote growth in understanding what we've been missing about God [within His word] and to foster relationships by knowing more about Him.

It is of necessity that you, the reader, understand that *What You Might Have Missed (Vol 1)* is in no way intended to add or subtract from the Bible, nor be a substitute for you attending your local church services (fellowshipping and serving with other believers and being fed the Word of God by a godly, reputable, and knowledgeable pastor or teacher). The purpose here is to provide expounded perspectives that will possibly challenge and provoke in-depth, meaningful, and respectful conversations among God's Church (as a whole) as well as nurture personal relationships with God. As John stated, "And there are also many other things that Jesus did, which if they were written one by one, I suppose that even the world itself could not contain the books that should be written. Amen." (John 21:25, NKJV); the same holds true with the Holy Spirit being active in our lives this very day, extending the works of Jesus. The stories of our lives further proclaim the gospel on a grander scale via word, deed, and purpose being fulfilled. Based on that knowledge alone, we can agree that there is so much more that God is saying, revealing, and sharing for the developing, comforting, and strengthening of believers and adding to the fold every day.

This and other forthcoming volumes of *What You Might Have Missed* will surely be keepsakes to use for better understanding of certain biblical scriptures –spiritually and in context– that many of us find mindboggling or view as enigmas. So, as you begin reading and delving into *What You Might Have Missed (Vol 1)*, do so with a ready-to-learn mindset and without being judgmental. There is guaranteed to be a gem or two that will surely significantly complement and/or impact your study of the Bible, making these readings worthwhile.

SECTION I

Genesis 1 - 11

GENESIS 1

Overview

Chapter one of the book of Genesis presents an extraordinary, supernatural chronological view of an introduction and the creations performed by God during a period of six days. Whether the time span of six days is either literal or figurative, it continues to be heavily debated among scholars, theologians, and Bible readers alike. Nonetheless, the six-day introduction and creations are identified as:

1. Day 1 (verses 3-5): Light
2. Day 2 (verses 6-8): Atmosphere / firmament
3. Day 3 (verses 9-13): Dry ground, grass, plants, and trees
4. Day 4 (verses 14-19): Lights (sun, moon & stars)
5. Day 5 (verses 20-23): Birds & sea creatures
6. Day 6 (verses 24-27): Livestock, creeping things, animals, & mankind

Scriptural Reading

¹In the beginning, God created the heavens and the earth. ²The earth was formless and empty. Darkness was on the surface of

the deep and God's Spirit was hovering over the surface of the waters.

[3]God said, "Let there be light," and there was light. [4]God saw the light and saw that it was good. God divided the light from the darkness. [5]God called the light "day", and the darkness he called "night". There was evening and there was morning, the first day.

[6]God said, "Let there be an expanse in the middle of the waters, and let it divide the waters from the waters." [7]God made the expanse and divided the waters which were under the expanse from the waters which were above the expanse; and it was so. [8]God called the expanse "sky". There was evening and there was morning, a second day.

[9]God said, "Let the waters under the sky be gathered together to one place, and let the dry land appear;" and it was so. [10]God called the dry land "earth", and the gathering together of the waters he called "seas". God saw that it was good. [11]God said, "Let the earth yield grass, herbs yielding seeds, and fruit trees bearing fruit after their kind, with their seeds in it, on the earth"; and it was so. [12]The earth yielded grass, herbs yielding seed after their kind, and trees bearing fruit, with their seeds in it, after their kind; and God saw that it was good. [13]There was evening and there was morning, a third day.

[14]God said, "Let there be lights in the expanse of the sky to divide the day from the night; and let them be for signs to mark seasons, days, and years; [15]and let them be for lights in the expanse of the sky to give light on the earth"; and it was so. [16]God made the two great lights: the greater light to rule the day, and the lesser light to rule the night. He also made the stars. [17]God set them in the expanse of the sky to give light to the earth, [18]and to rule over the day and over the night, and to divide the light from the darkness. God saw that it was good. [19]There was evening and there was morning, a fourth day.

[20]God said, "Let the waters abound with living creatures, and let birds fly above the earth in the open expanse of the sky." [21]God created the large sea creatures and every living creature that moves, with which the waters swarmed, after their kind,

and every winged bird after its kind. God saw that it was good. [22]God blessed them, saying, "Be fruitful, and multiply, and fill the waters in the seas, and let birds multiply on the earth." [23]There was evening and there was morning, a fifth day.

[24]God said, "Let the earth produce living creatures after their kind, livestock, creeping things, and animals of the earth after their kind"; and it was so. [25]God made the animals of the earth after their kind, and the livestock after their kind, and everything that creeps on the ground after its kind. God saw that it was good.

[26]God said, "Let's make man in our image, after our likeness. Let them have dominion over the fish of the sea, and over the birds of the sky, and over the livestock, and over all the earth, and over every creeping thing that creeps on the earth." [27]God created man in his own image. In God's image he created him; male and female he created them.

[28]God blessed them. God said to them, "Be fruitful, multiply, fill the earth, and subdue it. Have dominion over the fish of the sea, over the birds of the sky, and over every living thing that moves on the earth." [29]God said, "Behold, I have given you every herb yielding seed, which is on the surface of all the earth, and every tree, which bears fruit yielding seed. It will be your food. [30]To every animal of the earth, and to every bird of the sky, and to everything that creeps on the earth, in which there is life, I have given every green herb for food"; and it was so.

[31]God saw everything that he had made, and behold, it was very good. There was evening and there was morning, a sixth day.

Questions & Discoveries

Light vs Lights

Why did the creations of light occur on two of the seven days of creation (Genesis 1:3-5 & 14-16)?

It is understandable why many would perceive the introduction of light (verses 3-5) and the creation of lights (verses 14-16) as being synonymous, when the verses are read exactly as written. However, in reviewing the scriptural verses 14-16, it is clearly revealed that the creation of lights on day four refers to the sun, moon, and stars. Verses 17-18 further provide the purpose of their creation as being to give light to the earth, to provide light in the day and at night, and to divide the light from darkness. Furthermore, the very first light as identified in verses 3-5 wasn't made (e.g. combining things together) nor created (e.g. something produced for the first time). Instead, it was an introduction of something spoken by God. What is that something? The answer is found in Proverbs 8:12, 22-30:

> [12]"I, wisdom, have made prudence my dwelling. Find out knowledge and discretion."
> [22]"The LORD possessed me in the beginning of his work, before his deeds of old.
> [23]I was set up from everlasting, from the beginning, before the earth existed.
> [24]When there were no depths, I was born, when there were no springs abounding with water.
> [25]Before the mountains were settled in place, before the hills, I was born;
> [26]while as yet he had not made the earth, nor the fields, nor the beginning of the dust of the world.
> [27]When he established the heavens, I was there. When he set a circle on the surface of the deep,
> [28]when he established the clouds above, when the springs of the deep became strong,
> [29]when he gave to the sea its boundary, that the waters should not violate his commandment, when he marked out the foundations of the earth,
> [30]then I was the craftsman by his side. I was a delight day by day, always rejoicing before him…"

So then, to what was introduced and symbolically labeled as "light" in Genesis 1:3-5 is none other than "wisdom". The entire chapter of Proverbs 8 presents the excellence and origination of wisdom. Before anything could rightly and viably be made or created, wisdom (or light) was needed for orchestrating, balancing, and sustaining the creation to come. God provided it in the form of Him speaking – being His living word. That's right! The very word that He speaks is wisdom and it's where light and life derive. Today we have the privilege of personally experiencing God's wisdom by our belief in and acceptance of Jesus. In 1 Corinthians 1:24 and 30, Jesus is known as the wisdom of God:

> [24]"…but to those who are called, both Jews and Greeks, Christ is the power of God and the wisdom of God."
> [30]"Because of him, you are in Christ Jesus, who was made [i.e., presented] to us wisdom from God, and righteousness and sanctification, and redemption…"

in John 1:1-2, He [Jesus] is known as the Word of God:

> "In the beginning was the Word, and the Word was with God, and the Word was God."

and John 14:6 reveals Him [Jesus] as the way, the truth, and the life:

> "Jesus said to him 'I am the way, the truth, and the life…'"

It was necessary for wisdom to have its place as light in the midst of darkness or else a massive universal mess would have been created. That very wisdom symbolically communicated and labeled as 'light' in Genesis 1:3-5 possesses the ceaseless power to overcome, pierce through, and push back darkness as it brings forth life and brighter days. It wisely makes use of what is needed in moments of darkness, giving way for inspiration and hope.

It's also noteworthy that God literally and metaphorically depicts light as day and darkness as night. Both are something we can relate to, with light serving to encourage and present hope in and through dark times of depression, loneliness, helplessness, and hopelessness.

As you read the Bible, allow His word to be an ongoing work of wisdom in your life. It'll surely prepare the light within to strengthen, encourage, and guide you through moments of darkness.

Man in Our Image

What is meant by man being made in "our" image (Genesis 1:26 & 27)?

In Genesis 1:26 and 27, we read about God making man in "our" [God's] image. Before we explore the characteristics of image, let's first do a probe for understanding the "our" that is mentioned. For starters, realize that *our* is a pronoun referring to the God being. One may ask, "God being what?" My clarifying response would be, "God being who?" The term *God* as used here and frequently annotated throughout the Old Testament is translated from the masculine Hebrew plural noun, 'Ĕlôhîym. In the Hebrew language, 'Ĕlôhîym signifies "gods' or "deities" (AMG, 1991). By no means does this infer there being individual gods comprising a single god as some sort of multi-headed monster or a theatrical spectacle. The 'Ĕlôhîym [God] presented in the scriptural text of the Bible is what many Christians recognize and accept as the Trinity, which consists of the Father, Son, and Holy Spirit, operating and coexisting as one, interchangeably performing seemingly individual functions.

Let's view this from a natural perspective using "John Doe" as an example. For John to live a fully viable and functioning life, he must be equipped with the three entities of intelligence (a mind), expression (ability to communicate), and an influential will (authority). Though each entity serves a specific function, all three simultaneously are embedded in the makeup of John's character and ability. Likewise, 'Ĕlôhîym (the triune God) consists of (and represents) the Father (the intellectual mind of God), Son (the expressed living word of God), and Holy Spirit (God's influential will).

God the Father is signified by intelligence (mind). It's in the mind where intelligence is attained and measured by gathering, deciphering, and acting upon. The Father is the gatherer and possessor of all information because He is omniscient (Isaiah 40:13). The Father is the decipherer of all information, as evident by creation (Genesis 1:1 through Genesis 2:3). The Father acts in good faith because He is faithful to His promises (Psalm 71:22). The pure mind of God is perfect and unfathomable for any of us to ever fully comprehend. Romans 12:2 reads, "Don't be conformed to this world, but be transformed by the renewing of your mind, so that you may prove what is the good, well-pleasing, and perfect will of God." The power and success of our minds lies within our commitment to Him by us gathering, deciphering, and acting upon His will as contained within His word (i.e., the Bible), which is why it is of the utmost importance for us to renew our minds by the word of God. As believers, we're to have the mind of Christ (1 Corinthians 2:16).

God the Son exists as the expressed Word. John 1:1 affirms Jesus as being the Word of God. As the expressed Word of God goes forth, what was in the mind of God manifests in the natural, as proclaimed in Isaiah 55:11. By Jesus (the expressed Word) being the maker of all creation, we are assured of Him being omnipresent, as He has proclaimed that He is always with us (Matthew 28:20). John 1:14 further describes Jesus (the expressed Word) as being full of grace. Mark 8:2-3 provides an illustration of Jesus (the expressed Word) being driven by compassion. These few attributes display the character of Jesus (the expressed Word) set forth in purposeful actions.

Unfortunately, today the expressed words of most of us have little to no value and provide very poor examples of being Christ-like believers. Sadly, and ignorantly, many do not grasp how words have either positively or negatively impacted their lives and how they're viewed by others, which causes the Church overall to suffer in shame. In Matthew 5:37, there is a most powerful and wise piece of advice given which we can all benefit from, regarding what we speak and act upon. It simply states, "But let your 'Yes' be 'Yes' and your 'No' be 'No.' Whatever is more than these is of the evil one." So often we answer impulsively, oversell on commitments that we have no intent to deliver on, or are somehow hindered from delivering on due to issues with our time, abilities, and/or resources. What we speak and act upon reveal an image of who we represent. Communicated words

-what we say and act upon- are so influential that it is emphatically proclaimed in the bible that "Death and life are in the power of the tongue..." (Proverbs 18:21). We must refrain from anxious speaking, consider the cost of what we're preparing to speak, and make it a practice/habit of being true to our words as believers.

God the Holy Spirit is represented in the form of influential authority. Luke 1:35 proves the omnipotence of the Holy Spirit (influential authority) to do the impossible and unnatural in our lives just as it was done with Mary being pregnant with Jesus without natural human relations. Likewise, the Holy Spirit (influential authority) has the power to be the change in our lives by empowering us (Acts 1:8) and giving us a new and purposeful life (Romans 8:11 & 2 Corinthians 5:17). For someone to be filled with the Holy Spirit (God's influential authority), a surrendering must take place in order for the leading of the Holy Spirit to be established. Luke 4:1 state, "Jesus, full of the Holy Spirit, returned from the Jordan and was led by the Spirit into the wilderness..." Remember, Jesus is the manifested expressed Word of God. However, the power within Him as the expressed Word of the Father comes by the leadership of the Holy Spirit within.

John 15:26 proclaims the Holy Spirit (influential authority) as the Counselor and further shares of the Spirit testifying about Jesus (the expressed Word of God). As many of us know [or may not know], wise counsel interprets and makes relatable the bigger pieces of the puzzle to fit into our comprehension – meeting us where we are intellectually. Furthermore, according to Ephesians 3:16-19, the Holy Spirit (influential authority) strengthens our inner person so that we are able to bear His expressed Word (Jesus) living within us, to comprehend "the width and length and height and depth" of Christ's love, and to be filled with all the fullness of God. It enables us to realize that God didn't give us a spirit of fear, but of power, love, and self-control (2 Timothy 1:7). Lastly, the Holy Spirit (influential authority) employs discernment in our lives for understanding and making wise choices concerning good and evil (Hebrews 5:14).

So, how does this correlate to us being made in God's image? Simply put, when God created us in the beginning, we were created with natural abilities of intelligence, expression, and influence.

However, as we will see in Chapter 3, those abilities were relegated to capabilities because of sin entering our genetic makeup. We are beings who were created with and designed to use our minds, communicative skills, and influential will for the good while living on earth. What sets our image apart from reflecting God's image is sin. It is because of sin that we've become a predominantly entropic civilization, and continually drift further from the righteous and perfect image of God. Our minds have become polluted and governed by selfishness, separatist ideologies (elitism, fraternities, etc.), greed, and negativity. Because of sin, we have a propensity to express the opposite of being Christ-like. Now we've become the product of, and we promote whatever word it is that lives in us. Expressing ourselves has been diluted to the point of society becoming desensitized to and acceptable of hate, prejudices, injustices, untruths, immorality, and overlooking the well-being of others. Because of sin, there's been a surrendering of our influential will for living righteous as we hypnotically, powerlessly, and easily follow the ways of this world to our detriment – shamefully and obliviously, we are leading others down the same path.

GENESIS 2

Overview

Chapter two of the book of Genesis begins with the induction of the 7th day as the capstone of the first seven days. From there, the chapter begins a historical reflection which expounds upon significant events regarding creations within the seven days leading to God's established plan for mankind. The five discoveries are:

1. The Seventh Day (God rests?)
2. The Garden of Eden (What is the garden of Eden?)
3. The Tree of Life and the Tree of the Knowledge of Good and Evil (Why plant them in the garden? Why was the tree of the knowledge of good and evil deemed as good for food?)
4. The River(s) (What are the significances of the four rivers?)
5. The Creation of Woman (Why is woman made as a helper (help meet) comparable to man? Why did God cause the man to fall into a deep sleep?)

Scriptural Reading

^{1}The heavens, the earth, and all their vast array were finished. ^{2}On the seventh day God finished his work which he had done;

and he rested on the seventh day from all his work which he had done. [3]God blessed the seventh day, and made it holy, because he rested in it from all his work of creation which he had done.

[4]This is the history of the generations of the heavens and of the earth when they were created, in the day that the LORD God made the earth and the heavens. [5]No plant of the field was yet in the earth, and no herb of the field had yet sprung up; for the LORD God had not caused it to rain on the earth. There was not a man to till the ground, [6]but a mist went up from the earth, and watered the whole surface of the ground. [7]The LORD God formed man from the dust of the ground and breathed into his nostrils the breath of life; and man became a living soul. [8]The LORD God planted a garden eastward, in Eden, and there he put the man whom he had formed. [9]Out of the ground the LORD God made every tree to grow that is pleasant to the sight, and good for food, including the tree of life in the middle of the garden and the tree of the knowledge of good and evil. [10]A river went out of Eden to water the garden; and from there it was parted and became the source of four rivers. [11]The name of the first is Pishon: it flows through the whole land of Havilah, where there is gold; [12]and the gold of that land is good. Bdellium and onyx stone are also there. [13]The name of the second river is Gihon. It is the same river that flows through the whole land of Cush. [14]The name of the third river is Hiddekel. This is the one which flows in front of Assyria. The fourth river is the Euphrates.

[15]The LORD God took the man and put him into the garden of Eden to cultivate and keep it. [16]The LORD God commanded the man, saying, "You may freely eat of every tree of the garden; [17]but you shall not eat of the tree of the knowledge of good and evil; for in the day that you eat of it, you will surely die."

[18]The LORD God said, "It is not good for the man to be alone. I will make him a helper comparable to him." [19]Out of the ground the LORD God formed every animal of the field, and every bird of the sky, and brought them to the man to see what

he would call them. Whatever the man called every living creature became its name. [20]The man gave names to all livestock, and to the birds of the sky, and to every animal of the field; but for man there was not found a helper comparable to him. [21]The LORD God caused the man to fall into a deep sleep. As the man slept, he took one of his ribs and closed up the flesh in its place. [22]The LORD God made a woman from the rib which he had taken from the man and brought her to the man. [23]The man said, "This is now bone of my bones, and flesh of my flesh. She will be called 'woman,' because she was taken out of Man." [24]Therefore a man will leave his father and his mother, and will join with his wife, and they will be one flesh. [25]The man and his wife were both naked, and they were not ashamed.

Questions & Discoveries

The Seventh Day

God rests (Genesis 2:2-3)?

Looking at Genesis 2:1-3, we read about the establishment of the seventh day. What many have come to accept in reading these verses is the belief of it being a day in which God rested in the sense of Him relaxing and/or recovering. However, when careful attention is given to the word "rested" as used in verse 2, we find that it is not the typical rest often thought of (i.e., relax, recover, etc.). In the Hebrew language, the word used for "rested" is "shāvath", which means "to cease or stop". You may be thinking to yourself, "Well, isn't that the same as relaxing and/or recovering?" Not quite. Shāvath used here in verse 2 signifies God ceasing/stopping from creating anything any further outside the purpose of what He has already established (e.g. all creation). It does not mean He's sitting somewhere recovering or relaxing and not doing anything afterward. As a matter of fact, Psalm 121:4 states quite the opposite as it declares that He neither slumber nor sleep.

By God having nothing more to create at that time (the seventh day), He was therefore able to bless (bestow divine favor upon) the seventh day and set it apart from the other days in which His work had been completed. In other words, for God, this was a moment of appreciation taken in relation to time as we know it –the seventh day- signifying completeness. Oh, how great things would've been if sin had never entered the world which disturbed God's rest (cease) from work. For in the scriptures, we find that His creative work would resume in the process of us needing salvation (Romans 5:8 and 1 Peter 3:18) and the need for a new heaven and a new earth (Isaiah 65:17-19 and Revelation 21:1). Peace and harmony shall be in the new creation what God intended it to be in the beginning, an eternal seventh day of appreciation for us to enjoy with Him.

Garden of Eden

What is the garden of Eden (Genesis 2:8)?

According to Meriam-Webster dictionary (online), 'garden' is defined as, a plot of ground where herbs, fruits, flowers, or vegetables are cultivated; a rich well-cultivated region. In researching, you'll find that Eden is a Hebrew word that carries the connotation of paradise, pleasure, or delight. Scripturally we see the garden of Eden being a place where God planted trees that were pleasant to the sight and good for food as well as a place where He positioned man to manage and guard. In essence, the garden of Eden represented the heart (altar) of God which He entrusted to man. It was a place of worship (man's service to God), relationship (man walking with God), and ownership (man being entrusted with God's heart (altar)).

Metaphorically speaking, the garden of Eden was a spiritual place representing God having a righteous, harmonious relationship with mankind which was manifested in a physical, inherent, and sinless state. Simply put, the garden of Eden represented the loving heart and gracious mindset of God towards mankind as they basked in relationship with Him. The garden of Eden is somewhat reflected in the hearts of good and caring parents toward their children as a place where their needs are met, where they have no worries, where they genuinely reciprocate love and respect, and most importantly, where they hold true to words of instruction and wisdom from the parents. It's a harmonious place of joy, peace, and reverence -a safe space to be in without condemnation- with mutual understanding as to what is and what is not allowed, all for the good of a healthy and prosperous relationship with long life.

The Tree of Life and The Tree of The Knowledge of Good and Evil

Why plant and grow the tree of life and the tree of the knowledge of good and evil in the garden of Eden (Genesis 2:9)?

In Genesis 2:9, we find the first mention of God making every tree to grow, to include the tree of life and the tree of the knowledge of good and evil in the garden of Eden. What many often gloss over is the purpose of these words found in the same verse: "pleasant to the sight, and good for food" and "in the middle of the garden". You're probably wondering to yourself, "What am I missing?" and "Where are you going with this?" Put on your seatbelt and enjoy the scenery of the bigger picture being painted.

As believers, we all can attest to God being omniscient (all knowing) and that we were created to be in relationship with Him as His children. With that being the case, it would be fair to say that in His infinite wisdom, He knew and knows the power of Satan's contaminated, influential character as a liar and murderer (John 8:44), a thief (John 10:10) and a deceiver (Revelation 12:9). By God knowing all of that, He also knew (and knows) that Satan's priority would be (and is) to kill, steal, and destroy anything related to, like, and/or representing God – be it us and/or all creation. So, what did He (God) do in Genesis 2:9 to combat Satan's anticipated strategy? He set in motion His redemptive plan for mankind. In the garden of Eden, He put trees in place that were pleasant to the eye, pleasant for food, and in rightful positions (with the tree of life being in the middle of the garden, and the tree of the knowledge of good and evil being elsewhere in the garden). Before sin entered the scene, mankind

15

(being in a right relationship with God) viewed and appreciated the trees the same as God did/does and out of a trust in His instructions, they obeyed for a time.

With God having created mankind and given him free will, and Him having undeniable love for mankind, He provided for their needs as well as gave them specific instructions to be acted upon. Just as any good and caring parent, God would like for His children to follow wise instruction for their good, but He also knew (and knows) that genuine reciprocated love can only be expressed by free will from the heart. For free will to be enacted, mankind must be presented with facts. Hence, the tree of life and the tree of the knowledge of good and evil come into play. The tree of life is what God says it is, the tree of life (representing the eternal, central focus of paradise rooted in a right, harmonious relationship with God). Remember what was stated earlier regarding God being omniscient and setting in motion His redemptive plan? Well, the tree of life served as a Christophany (i.e., a manifested depiction or form representing Christ) just as many other objects throughout the Bible (e.g., pillar of cloud by day, pillar of fire by night, burning bush, etc.). It came into play here in the garden of Eden and will resume its position in Revelation 22. Take notice regarding the tree of life having been planted and grown in the center of the garden, whereas the tree of the knowledge of good and evil being grown in the garden but not in the center. The tree of life is grounded in and obtained by faith – the centerpiece of mankind's eternal and right relationship with God.

Some of us may be thinking how great it would've been if that was the only tree for mankind to select. However, please make no mistake in thinking that the tree of the knowledge of good and evil was something God should not have allowed in the garden of Eden. First, it is imperative that we understand that God operates within the heart of people (1 Chronicles 28:9). With that knowledge and accepting the garden of Eden as being symbolic of God's heart, it was only right that He permitted both trees in the garden for providing truthful and wise instruction, the same choices we have, and our hearts must rightly discern for our living. God knew (and knows) the arsenal of the enemy will be used to manipulate mankind's free will

– attempting to permanently sever the relationship between God and man. What Satan did not count on was the very tree he figured would kill man's relationship with God was really being used to expose him and his nature.

As illustrated in verses 15 through 17, we witness God placing man in the garden of Eden to maintain it and instructing him to freely eat of every tree except the tree of the knowledge of good and evil (failure to do so would result in death). The Hebrew word for 'knowledge' is "dha'ath" and it means moral cognition and to gain knowledge through the senses (i.e., works, experiences). The tree of the knowledge of good and evil was not placed in the garden as a choice for us but as a warning and deterrence for us to avoid death in doing works toward a relationship with God.

Now, little did man know that in time Satan would slither his way in and create a huge problem resulting in dire ramifications. As we would find out in Chapter 3, Satan took notice of the ability of the sensations to influence mankind (seeing what was pleasant to the eye, pleasant for food, and in rightful positions) and set out with a plan of distortion to introduce and refocus mankind's sensations towards the lust of the flesh, the lust of the eyes, and the pride of life (1 John 2:16) by using fruit from the tree of the knowledge of good and evil.

So, to answer the leading question "Why plant and grow the tree of life and the tree of the knowledge of good and evil in the garden of Eden?", we find the answer being twofold. First, as an illustration of the truth before us (life and death), and properly preparing us in making wise decisions. Secondly, to represent how we're to rightly discern, know, and grow in a right relationship with God by understanding, appreciating, and accepting that which is pleasant to the eye (salvation in Jesus), good for food (trusting the word of God), and in the middle of the garden (being humble before God) rather than seeking a relationship with Him through works and/or displacing Him entirely by feeding the lust of the flesh, lust of the eye, and the pride of life. Today, we still contend with whether to accept the tree of life (Jesus) or the tree of knowledge of good and evil (doing things our way). And, for many, the vices of Satan (i.e., lust of the eyes, lust of the flesh, and pride of life) win.

Why was the tree of the knowledge of good and evil deemed as "good for food" (Genesis 2:9 & 17)?

In examining what the Hebrew word is and it's meaning behind the word "good", we find that in Hebrew it is "Tōv" which means pleasant, delightful, correct, etc. So, yes, it was good for food, but it was not good for the consumption by those walking with God due to the curse that comes with it (as identified in Romans 1:28-32), which is why God instructed man not to partake of it (Genesis 2:17). There's a cliché that goes like this, "Not all money is good money". What makes the fruit of the tree of the knowledge of good and evil good for food is that it feeds the mentality of self-centeredness, shame, guilt, etc. and matures one in the ways of the devil, to believe false narratives which contradict God's standards of truth, holiness, and righteousness. Just like any natural garden, what grows there is based on what is planted and allowed there by the owner. The hopeful result is always for good to abound within the confines of the garden; however, it's dependent on everyone doing their part. More will be discussed on this topic in Chapter 3.

The River(s)

What is the significance of the four rivers (Genesis 2:10-14)?

Interestingly, we read in Genesis 2:10-14 about an unnamed river watering Eden and flowing from there, splintering into four other rivers which are named. Let's look at these verses in two parts with the first addressing the unnamed river and the second deciphering the four splintered rivers. One truth many of us learned in grade school biology classes is that survival is based on the necessity of water. Water is fundamental to life in that it serves multiple purposes which are beneficial to every living creature, thing, and place. Without water, droughts, famines, sicknesses, and even death would prevail. What's special about the unnamed river which watered Eden is that the verses do not identify from whence the water came. As a matter of fact, the only early scripture reference regarding water at the time of and for the garden of Eden is Genesis 2:6 where it mentions a mist coming up from the earth to water the ground. So, that negates the belief that there was already an established river in place.

Let's put our thinking caps on and dig a little deeper to search out a reservoir of reason. Remember in Genesis 1 where we read and learned about the trinity and, in particular, the Holy Spirit being God's influential will, and in the previous discussion where we learned about the garden of Eden representing the heart of God? Guess what? That unnamed river mentioned in Genesis 2:10 correlates with the eternal life-giving water in Eden. It was a self-sustaining headwater which provided life throughout the heart of God (i.e., Eden) and from the heart God (i.e., Eden). As a matter of fact, pertaining to a conversation between Jesus and a woman at the well, we read these profound verses in John 4:

[13] Jesus answered her, "Everyone who drinks of this water will thirst again, [14] but whoever drinks of the water that I will give him will never thirst again; but the water that I will give him will become in him a well of water springing up to eternal life."

Isn't it interesting that the river that watered Eden is comparable to that which lives in and extends from Christ? Both are life giving sources without a beginning nor an ending. Yes, the unnamed river was a true-life body of water, but most importantly it was metaphorically a representation of the Holy Spirit.

Now that the foundation has been laid for the unnamed river, we can now address the main question of, "What is the significance of the four rivers mentioned in Genesis 2:13-14?" The short answer is they metaphorically illustrate an overflowing of God's grace in providing, nourishing, and extending hope to all creation, things, and places living outside a right relationship with God. In Matthew 5:45 Jesus states, "…He makes His sun to rise on the evil and the good, and sends rain on the just and the unjust."

Take note of how all four splintered rivers are mentioned by name (Pishon, Gihon, Hiddekel, and Euphrates), juxtaposing the unnamed river. Remarkably each river's name carries an etymological meaning in the Hebrew language which represents expressed characteristics of the unnamed river. Reading further, you'll find that these rivers are still active today in our lives as witnesses to God's presence, grace, and mercy. Let's delve deeper by piecing the puzzle together.

The first river mentioned is Pishon which means "jump", "bounce", or "increase". It streams through the land of Havilah which means 'circle' in Hebrew. Havilah is said to be the land where there is good gold, bdellium, and onyx stones. In other words, it's a rich and beautiful place. There's nothing wrong with the riches one possesses but when it becomes the circle (and/or cycle) of our pursuit, God sends a graceful dosage of His Spirit (Pishon) to jump start, bounce back, and/or increase our awareness of His presence.

The second river mentioned is Gihon which means 'burst forth'. It streams through the land of Cush which translates to "dark". Cush (or dark) represents a place of unconsciousness or gloomy pessimism. It's a place where many live in despair and hopelessness. However, God sends a graceful dosage of His Spirit (Gihon) to nourish and provide an opportunity for a bursting forth of encouragement as a reminder of His mercy and presence.

The third river mentioned is Hiddekel which means "rapid" or "swift". It streams in front of the land of Assyria which stands for "the god". Assyria is a place where anything and anyone can be viewed as a god. Yet, God sends an urgent and graceful dosage of His Spirit (Hiddekel) to quickly call us to Him, reminding us that He's the priority and one true God, with open arms, being full of grace, mercy, and love.

The fourth and final river mentioned is Euphrates which means "fruitfulness". It is a standalone river which is known for being a great river (Revelation 9:14 and 16:12). Euphrates symbolizes a great and mighty outpouring dosage of God's Holy Spirit that is provided for the "whosoever will" as penned in Mark 8:34 and Revelation 22:19. It serves as a call for transformation, a quenching of our thirst, and a producing of fruit in our lives (as depicted in Galatians 5:22-23).

These splintered four rivers all flowed from one source – the unnamed river. It was the unnamed river which originated and encapsulated the powerful characteristics apportioned to each of the splintered rivers, just as it provided within the garden of Eden what was necessary for the growth of the trees (including the tree of the knowledge of good and evil). That's the goodness of God!

The Creation of Woman

Why is woman made as a helper (help meet) comparable for man (Genesis 2:18)?

In answering this lead question, its simple answer was provided by God in the problem statement: "It is not good for the man to be alone." Recognizing the problem, He then follows up with a solution statement – "I will make him a helper comparable to him." Now that we've identified the clarity of the woman being made, let's "peel back the onion" to get to the core of woman's creation according to God's plan. In Genesis 2:18, we see the phrase "a helper comparable to him." The original Hebrew phrase is "ezer kenegedo" and it is also translated as "a helper fit for him," "a helper as his counterpart," and "help meet" (being the most common). For this discovery, we're going to focus on the translation 'a helper comparable to him' because it contains the key word "comparable", which is most appropriate for addressing who God was providing to man.

According to the Oxford language dictionary (online), comparable is defined as 'of equivalent quality; worthy of comparison.' What makes this intriguing is understanding God's standard for man's helper (or help meet). This individual was to be created with the equivalent qualities which complement and uphold a certain level of value to the man. Specifically, she was to represent the man as his ambassador, with qualities of being loyal and like-minded in comprehension, while possessing and exercising free will with respect to the man – just like the reflection of man being made in the image of God. As man walked with, honored, and respected God, she was to do the same with the man (Ephesians 5:22-24 and 33).

See, there is a tremendous difference between having a comparable mate and having a compatible one. Too often, men seek women who are compatible rather than comparable. The difference being that a woman found to be comparable draws a complementary comparison as she respects and represents him well and in loyalty; whereas a woman found to be compatible focuses on her satisfying a need. When we wait on God, He has a way of fashioning the woman comparable for the man, just as He connected Ruth and Boaz (read the book of Ruth in the Bible) and just as Proverbs 31:10-31 provides a descriptive model of a virtuous woman.

Why did God cause the man to fall into a deep sleep (Genesis 2:21-22)?

In reading the key scriptures (Genesis 2:21-22) for the lead question, we find there to be a treasure chest of wisdom which clues us in on God's way of thinking when it comes to provision. Take a brief moment to read or reflect on God's creations during the first six days in Genesis 1. Notice how the creations of each day were made to support the creations of the following day. Now take a look again at Genesis 2:18, with concentration on the statement, "It is not good for the man to be alone." The implication throughout Genesis 1 and in Genesis 2:18 is that God is mindful of all things that were and are needed. What is needed for tomorrow, He's already planned for it coming to pass. Oftentimes, we allow anxiety, greed, lust, emotions, and pride to push us into something we are/were not ready for (we'll leave that there for another teaching at another time). However, the point here is knowing and accepting that God knows our needs.

In Genesis 2:21, we read that God "caused" the man to fall into a "deep sleep." Very interesting information to uncover here. The word "caused" is translated from the Hebrew word "Naphal" which means "to fall, lie, position". The phrase "deep sleep" is translated from the Hebrew word "Tardēmâh" which means "trance". Understand that being in a trance carries the connotation of being in a deep sleep, as though under a spell, in which a person is unable to exercise normal reactions and unable to comprehend awareness of what is taking place. So, to rephrase the statement made in Genesis 2:21 in plain language, we can read it as "God positioned man to be in a heavily tranquil state."

Now, in the natural we plainly understand that man was in an anesthetic state to any feelings or awareness. This was needed as part of God's plan for bringing out of man what He'd already placed in mankind on the sixth day of creation (hence, when He created mankind). Remember, the seventh day was the day He stopped creating anything any further, which was simply because every living creature had the ability to reproduce. The difference with man is that his comparable mate had to be extracted (not created) and made (formed) from his very being in order for them (he and she) to reproduce. The template and cycle of reproduction was already in God's plan just as He had stated for the plants, livestock, fish, and all other living creatures in Genesis 1. It was in the deep sleep that God was able to form the first medical operation, delivering from man and to man his comparable mate.

Another valuable piece of information that jumps out in this process of how God works in fulfilling needs, is how He provides for our needs based on His will and timing, which most often occurs when we're unaware. It brings to mind Matthew 6:25-30, where Jesus encourages His disciples against being anxious and directs them to depend on God, who knows our needs and will provide for them. Surely, if He can pull from man and form a woman, He can pull His promises, ideas, and abilities out of us, making a way when there seemingly wasn't a way, as we remain in faith and planted and watered by His word.

GENESIS 3

Overview

Chapter three of the book of Genesis provides us with actual details regarding mankind's sin of disobedience (which severed the right, harmonious relationship they had with God), consequences to bear because of the sin, and exile from the garden of Eden. Though one may perceive this chapter as one of gloom and doom, it turns out to be an endearing testament of God's love, grace, and mercy toward mankind. In this chapter, we'll discuss and examine the following five discoveries:

1. Was the tree of the knowledge of good and evil in the middle of the garden?
2. Why and when did the woman eat from the forbidden tree?
3. Was woman's penalty for sin centered only on married women and women who were able to bear children and not for single and childless women?
4. Is it wrong for woman to 'desire' her husband and for him to 'rule' over her?
5. What is the significance of the names 'Woman' and 'Eve'?

Scriptural Reading

[1]Now the serpent was more subtle than any animal of the field which the LORD God had made. He said to the woman, "Has God really said, 'You shall not eat of any tree of the garden?'" [2]The woman said to the serpent, "We may eat fruit from the trees of the garden, [3]but not the fruit of the tree which is in the middle of the garden. God has said, 'You shall not eat of it. You shall not touch it, lest you die.'" [4]The serpent said to the woman, "You won't really die, [5]for God knows that in the day you eat it, your eyes will be opened, and you will be like God, knowing good and evil." [6]When the woman saw that the tree was good for food, and that it was a delight to the eyes, and that the tree was to be desired to make one wise, she took some of its fruit, and ate. Then she gave some to her husband with her, and he ate it, too. [7]Their eyes were opened, and they both knew that they were naked. They sewed fig leaves together, and made coverings for themselves. [8]They heard the LORD God's voice walking in the garden in the cool of the day, and the man and his wife hid themselves from the presence of the LORD God among the trees of the garden. [9]The LORD God called to the man, and said to him, "Where are you?" [10]The man said, "I heard your voice in the garden, and I was afraid, because I was naked; so I hid myself." [11]God said, "Who told you that you were naked? Have you eaten from the tree that I commanded you not to eat from?" [12]The man said, "The woman whom you gave to be with me, she gave me fruit from the tree, and I ate it." [13]The LORD God said to the woman, "What have you done?" The woman said, "The serpent deceived me, and I ate." [14]The LORD God said to the serpent,"Because you have done this,you are cursed above all livestock,and above every animal of the field.You shall go on your belly and you shall eat dust all the days of your life.

¹⁵I will put hostility between you and the woman, and between your offspring and her offspring. He will bruise your head, and you will bruise his heel."

¹⁶To the woman he said, "I will greatly multiply your pain in childbirth. You will bear children in pain. Your desire will be for your husband, and he will rule over you."

¹⁷To Adam he said, "Because you have listened to your wife's voice, and have eaten from the tree, about which I commanded you, saying, 'You shall not eat of it,' the ground is cursed for your sake. You will eat from it with much labor all the days of your life.

¹⁸It will yield thorns and thistles to you; and you will eat the herb of the field.

¹⁹You will eat bread by the sweat of your face until you return to the ground, for you were taken out of it. For you are dust, and you shall return to dust."

²⁰The man called his wife Eve because she would be the mother of all the living.

²¹The LORD God made garments of animal skins for Adam and for his wife, and clothed them.

²²The LORD God said, "Behold, the man has become like one of us, knowing good and evil. Now, lest he reach out his hand, and also take of the tree of life, and eat, and live forever—"

²³Therefore the LORD God sent him out from the garden of Eden, to till the ground from which he was taken. ²⁴So he drove out the man; and he placed cherubim at the east of the garden of Eden, and a flaming sword which turned every way, to guard the way to the tree of life.

Questions & Discoveries

The Tree in the Middle of the Garden

Was the tree of the knowledge of good and evil in the middle of the garden (Genesis 3:3)?

As discussed in Genesis 2:9, we examined that the tree of life was planted in the middle of the garden of Eden whereas the tree of the knowledge of good and evil was planted in the garden (not necessarily in the middle). So, your question may be, "Well, why does the woman state the tree of the knowledge of good and evil as being in the middle of the garden in Genesis 3:3?" Let's answer by examining a couple of items beginning with what is found in Genesis 3:1.

Firstly, take note of how the serpent is described as being more "subtle" than any beast of the field. According to Meriam-Webster dictionary (online), subtle is defined as "making use of clever and indirect methods to achieve something". Grasping that definition sheds light on the devil (working through the serpent) being not only skillful at extracting and distorting information but also for gauging and refocusing the mind and attention of his prey. Doing such allows for the victim's defeat by their oblivious concession to the enemy's deception.

Secondly, let's look at the prepositional phrase 'Has God really said' which he (the serpent) used when posing and sowing the question of doubt with the woman in Genesis 3:1. That phrase implies the devil has previously heard what he's questioning. Question for you. Was he (the serpent) repeating what was told to him by God or by the man? Scripturally, what we know is that whenever God has personally spoken with mankind, Satan was not privy to such conversations. With that being the case, I lean toward it being the man whom the devil heard the information from based on 1 Timothy 2:14 stating, "Adam wasn't deceived, but the woman, being deceived, has fallen into disobedience". Is it fair to say that for Adam not to be deceived there had to be an opportunity afforded him to be deceived? If so (which I strongly believe is the case), that opportunity had to have come by the devil (through the serpent). Speculatively but strongly probable, he (the devil) may have slyly inquired of the man, through general conversation, about what was prohibited by God and the man may have nonchalantly shared but stood strong and convincingly firm on God's instruction regarding the tree of the knowledge of good and evil. Not able to gain a footing with the man, the serpent took the information he received from the man, repackaged it, and used it as ammunition when he seized the opportunity to discreetly and skillfully challenge the woman's loyalty to obedience. In doing so, he was able to gain the footing needed toward severing the relationship between God and man with hopes of totally destroying God's creation.

Finally, as we circle back to answering the lead question, understand that it was the tree of life planted in the center of the garden of Eden whereas the tree of the knowledge of good and evil was planted somewhere in the garden (but not in the middle), as previously expounded upon in Genesis 2. How the woman was able to see the tree of the knowledge of good and evil as being in the middle is when it became the focus of her attention by the enemy redirecting her focus toward it. So, it wasn't that the tree was planted in the middle of the garden, but it was seen as such when it became the woman's center focus, clouding her spiritual and mental bearing. It's the same issue that most of us face today, spiritually and in the natural. We know and seek to please God by partaking of His word in solemn obedience; however, when a seed of doubt is allowed in and entertained, it then becomes the center of our attention. Before we know it, we're now wavering and walking outside the will of God as we trade the tree of life for unplanned, tumultuous experiences.

When She Ate the Fruit

Why did the woman eat from the forbidden tree (Genesis 3:1-6)?

Many of us can attest to the fact of knowing whoever controls the conversation can easily influence the other's thinking. So was the case during the dialog between the serpent and the woman. Approaching under the guise of having a harmless conversation, each word he spoke was shrewdly fueling the woman's doubt of God's word which eventually led to the woman eating from the forbidden tree.

Let's dissect what led to the woman eating from the tree of the knowledge of good and evil. The serpent used one tactical question to accomplish three goals fitting his ultimate plan of destruction. In Genesis 3:1 we read, "Has God really said, 'You shall not eat of any tree of the garden?'" That one question allowed the serpent to perform surveillance on how much the woman knew, gauge her interest, and sow a seed of doubt. In her response (Genesis 3:2-3), his surveillance proved that not only did the woman know what God had said but she didn't mind exaggerating on what He said by her adding "You shall not touch it" – which may have been a show of resentment or dissent on her part. Her response opened the door for the serpent to sow a seed of doubt and capitalize on her emotions. Even the devil (through the serpent) knew that God said no such thing about touching the tree. As a matter of fact, when he responded to her, he did not make any mention of touching the tree and only addressed eating from the tree. That slip of the lip by the woman told him all he needed to know in going forward with his mission. Notice the doubt instigated as he replied in Genesis 3:4, "You won't really die…" as well as the enticement of her emotions with his statement "…for God knows that in the day you eat it, your eyes will be opened, and you will be like God, knowing good and evil (Genesis 3:5)."

Notwithstanding, the temptation was too great for her to bear in her own strength as her mind and flesh willingly joined forces with the words of the serpent in usurping the man's authoritative role and God's word (Genesis 3:6). Cunningly, the devil managed to obstruct her view and misguide her emotions from what God had created as pleasant to the eye, pleasant for food, and in rightful positions to seeing and accepting the tree of the knowledge of good and evil in the middle of the garden for satisfying her lust of the flesh, lust of the eye, and pride of life (as identified in 1 John 2:16).

When was the forbidden fruit eaten (Genesis 3:5-8)?

When reading Genesis 3:4-8, it's easy to hold to the idea that the conversation between the serpent and the woman, the woman eating the fruit, the woman's and man's eyes being opened, and them covering themselves with fig leaves all occurred successively on the same day. However, what if that wasn't the case? Could it be that we're missing a show of God's grace? If that can be proven as the case, could it possibly change some mindsets and anxieties regarding the notion that God operates instantaneously and is ready to judge us for wrong doings? Well, let's analyze Genesis 3:4-8 and sort out the embedded discoveries.

Beginning with Genesis 3:5, we see that the serpent is speaking to the woman. During his monologue, he says something pretty interesting being: "for God knows that in the day you eat it". Upon closer observation you will notice the prepositional phrase "in the day", which carries the same connotation as "when" and "as soon as" – implying future tense as in not necessarily now but in time. What the serpent was doing is simply planting the seed and as many of us know seeds take time to produce. Take note of how the serpent said what he had to say and was not seen nor heard of again until Genesis 3:13 which was well after the woman and the man had eaten the fruit, noticed one another's nakedness, and sewed fig leaves to cover themselves. Once he sowed his seeds of doubt, greed, and pride, he went about his way and allowed for his seeds to ponder in the mind of the woman.

In Genesis 3:6, we find the "when" (signifying the serpent's mention of 'in the day') coming into fruition. Upon his seed settling and growing in her mind after some time, she was compelled to act on it. More than likely, she never discussed with the man the conversation which took place between her and the serpent but chose to wrestle with it on her own to the point of her giving into the temptation of seeing and reaching to achieve the image which the devil painted in her mind. Some may ask, "How can you say she never discussed the conversation with the man?" Easily, because in Genesis 3:12, the man identified her as the source of reason for disobeying God and made no mention of the serpent. It wasn't until God had questioned the woman that the truth came forth. That also confirms that the man was not with her during her conversation with the serpent, but they were together at a later time when she took from the tree and shared with him.

At the time the man had partaken of the fruit (coming in agreement with the woman to do so), his natural abilities of intelligence, expression, and influence became warped (as discussed in Chapter 1 – 'Man in Our Image') which now left them in a state of being capable of attaining such an image again rather than having the natural abilities – it's what we contend with today. In answering the lead question, the forbidden fruit was eaten after the seeds of doubt, greed, and pride were planted and pondered over a period of time in the woman's mind.

At the opening of this reading, it was mentioned that there was a show of God's grace within these few verses (Genesis 3:5-8). During the time of the woman pondering on what the serpent had said (Genesis 3:6), she was in a period of God's grace where she could've shared what the serpent said with her husband in order to get her mind back on track to where it needed to be. However, she allowed her emotions to cloud her loyalty and discernment of God's word which resulted in her doing exactly what the devil wanted. Then, when she gave some of the fruit to the man, he allowed his emotions to cloud his authoritative position, loyalty to and trust of God's word. It was afterward, that instead of them capitalizing on a period of God's grace to seek Him for making things right during their initial time in sin, they instead attempted to fix things by covering themselves and hiding from God. Those are periods of His grace that we can all relate to. We think He's too upset with us or that we've messed up too badly that it's beyond the point of repairing our relationship with Him – nothing can be further from the truth. The grace He affords us is because of His love for us and is used to save us from further destruction.

Woman's Woes

Was Eve's penalty for sin centered only on married women and women who were able to bear children and not for single and childless women (Genesis 3:16)?

The consequence of sin is oftentimes thought of as only affecting the perpetrator of the transgression. Although that can be correct in some cases, it isn't for most. Please understand that the ramification of sin runs very broad and very deep. The fallout of sin in our lives can affect every aspect of our being to include spiritual, physical, mental, etc. as well as those we're connected to. The consequences generally set things off-balance in our lives including our relationship with others. Galatians 5:9 states it this way, "A little yeast grows through the whole lump."

When the man and woman first committed sin by eating the forbidden fruit, it opened the door for everything imaginable and unimaginable to be birthed through their being (of the flesh) and outside the will of God. As tough as it may be to understand and accept, men and women were not initially created with the flaw of being alone nor the inability to reproduce. In the beginning before sin entered in, woman was created for man and they were comparable (Genesis 2:18), and they were created and commanded to reproduce (Genesis 1:28) as husband and wife (Genesis 2:24). What sin did was take the God inspired nature of man and woman and metamorphosize it into the foreign nature we've been exemplifying ever since.

The results of Adam and Eve's sin set in motion the imbalanced population of men and women, the defects of experiencing infertility, women not wanting to experience pregnancy, different ideologies regarding family structure, the disconnect of men being fathers, etc. Some of these conditions are because of the genetic or hereditary flaw in the physiological and biological make up of our sinful bodies; some are mentally by choice; and some are spiritually brought on by others – however, the sinful nature of mankind serves as the basis for all.

So, why did God specifically call out the married and childbearing women in Genesis 3:16? It's nothing more than God showing they weren't exempt from the effects of sin although they have a form of godliness (in principle, being married and having children as fashioned during pre-sin times). Please understand that for a woman not to have a husband and/or bear children was heavily frowned upon from the very introduction of sin and up until nowadays. Being able to be married and conceive a child was considered (and is) an honorable blessing that many women longed for. However, with pride being a sin which quickly leads to an "I'm better than you" attitude, God (in His infinite wisdom) saw fit to cover all the bases upfront. Make no mistake about it, every creature bears the result of sin in some form or fashion. This is affirmed in Romans 5:12 which reads, "Therefore, as sin entered into the world through one man, and death through sin, so death passed to all men because all sinned."

Is it wrong for woman to "desire" her husband and for him to "rule" over her (Genesis 3:16)?

Let's briefly examine the background as to why God stated that the woman would "desire" her husband and he would "rule" over her. God's penalty for sin justly fits the crime. It's not that He personally inflicts the consequences dealt upon us. When we sin, He simply reveals what the consequences are now that we've stepped outside of His will and into the will of either the enemy or self. Stepping out of His will means that we're breaking a covenant with Him by rejecting what He offers for our good, such as peace, protection, love, etc. In the situation of the man and woman sinning in the garden, they relinquished their position, image, and loyalty to Him. Their position was relinquished when they ran and hid from Him instead of to Him. Their image (His likeness) was relinquished when they disobeyed by partaking of the forbidden fruit. Their loyalty to Him was relinquished when the word of the serpent was placed above His word of caution.

When they surrendered their position, image, and loyalty, they received the wages of death. For the married and childbearing woman, those wages included pain in childbirth, a desire for her husband, and the husband ruling over her. The pain in childbirth is symbolic to the pain God experienced in the birth of sin upon the man and the woman in the garden of Eden (His heart). Because the married and childbearing woman initiated the sinful act, it was just that she feels the pain of God's heart.

What has stumped many of us is the attempt to understand how it is considered a "bad" thing or penalty for the woman to 'desire' her husband and for him to "rule" over her. The Hebrew word for "desire" is "Teshuqah" and it means "to long after". Remember the previous statement regarding God's penalty being just? The enemy (through the serpent) longed after the fall and destruction of mankind by questioning and using enticing, manipulative words to get her (ultimately, them) to follow

34

sensationalized fleshly wants in accomplishing his goal. With her giving into what the enemy supplanted by awakening her flesh, she underwent a new birth process which now identifies her with the trickery of the enemy. Now to lay it out plainly, God was saying what caused you to fall is now a part of you – the longing after. The meaning behind her "desiring" her husband is her questioning and using enticing, manipulative words to get her husband to give into her demands and wants, in a negative sense.

The second part of the justly imposed judgment against the woman was her husband "ruling" over her. The Hebrew for "rule" is "Mashal" and it means "to have dominion". Remember in God's original plan for the man and the woman, it was for her to be comparable with him and for her to help him in exercising dominion over all the creatures and the earth. Now because of the woman taking advice from the serpent (a creature they were both given dominion over), her God-given and ordained position alongside her husband was jeopardized which resulted in her having to be under his dominion whenever she exercised the characteristics of "desire" as portrayed by the devil through the serpent. Remember, the man's authority was never surrendered because he did not give into the serpent, but she did.

Another Name

What is the significance of the names "Woman" (Genesis 2:23) and "Eve" (Genesis 3:20)?

It's a very interesting revelation as to why Adam called her "woman" in Genesis 2:23 and after the act of sin, he called her "Eve". Let's take a look at Genesis 2:23 as it reads, "The man said, 'This is now bone of my bones, and flesh of my flesh. She will be called 'woman,' because she was taken out of man." As woman, she identified with every aspect of what complemented the man – she was fashioned as comparable in all ways. There was no flaw in or about her and she came directly from the man and was presented to the man by God Himself.

As we read on in Genesis 3:20, it reads, "The man called his wife Eve because she would be the mother of all the living." Many may view this as being nothing of significance and consider it to be a good name in general. However, traditionally anytime someone was given a name, it represented something about their character, which serves as the basis for her new name. For Adam renaming the woman Eve, he was identifying her as the producer of all offspring born after the fallen nature of mankind as opposed to the God-inspired nature of the man and the woman prior to sin. No longer did he identify her as being comparable and being created and fashioned by God for him. Adam came to see her apart from himself due to the judgmental sin nature he now possessed. For him, this new birth of knowing good and evil presented reason enough for him to now judgmentally see her as the mother of all the living – meaning those coming forth under the sinful nature.as opposed to God's birthing of a living soul inspired by His breath of life as shown in Genesis 2:7.

GENESIS 4

Overview

This chapter marks the start of mankind's lineage through Adam and Eve after the fall and them (Adam and Eve along with their offspring) having to live life through their accursed sin nature, which we continue to contend with today. It's in this chapter where we read and learn about Cain and Abel (which many of us learned about in Sunday school) and what transpired to cause the first physical murder recorded in the Bible. What we'll come to find as being more intriguing is God's enduring mercy extended toward Cain as well as His loving grace shown toward Adam and Eve in the form of Seth. In this chapter, we'll discuss and examine the following discoveries:

1. Why was Abel and his offering respected by God but not Cain and his offering?
2. How was Cain able to rule over sin by committing sin?
3. How was Cain's penalty for sin justly comparable to the sin he committed?
4. Why did God mark Cain (a murderer) to protect his life from being taken?
5. What is the significance of Lamech proclaiming vengeance of his own volition?

6. What is the significance of Cain and Enoch in contrast to Abel and Enosh?

Scriptural Reading

[1]The man knew Eve his wife. She conceived, and gave birth to Cain, and said, "I have gotten a man with the LORD's help." [2]Again she gave birth, to Cain's brother Abel. Abel was a keeper of sheep, but Cain was a tiller of the ground. [3]As time passed, Cain brought an offering to the LORD from the fruit of the ground. [4]Abel also brought some of the firstborn of his flock and of its fat. The LORD respected Abel and his offering, [5]but he didn't respect Cain and his offering. Cain was very angry, and the expression on his face fell. [6]The LORD said to Cain, "Why are you angry? Why has the expression of your face fallen? [7]If you do well, won't it be lifted up? If you don't do well, sin crouches at the door. Its desire is for you, but you are to rule over it." [8]Cain said to Abel, his brother, "Let's go into the field." While they were in the field, Cain rose up against Abel, his brother, and killed him.
[9]The LORD said to Cain, "Where is Abel, your brother?" He said, "I don't know. Am I my brother's keeper?"
[10]The LORD said, "What have you done? The voice of your brother's blood cries to me from the ground. [11]Now you are cursed because of the ground, which has opened its mouth to receive your brother's blood from your hand. [12]From now on, when you till the ground, it won't yield its strength to you. You will be a fugitive and a wanderer in the earth."
[13]Cain said to the LORD, "My punishment is greater than I can bear. [14]Behold, you have driven me out today from the surface of the ground. I will be hidden from your face, and I will be a fugitive and a wanderer in the earth. Whoever finds me will kill me."
[15]The LORD said to him, "Therefore whoever slays Cain, vengeance will be taken on him sevenfold." The LORD appointed a sign for Cain, so that anyone finding him would not strike him.

¹⁶Cain left the LORD's presence, and lived in the land of Nod, east of Eden. ¹⁷Cain knew his wife. She conceived and gave birth to Enoch. He built a city and named the city after the name of his son, Enoch. ¹⁸Irad was born to Enoch. Irad became the father of Mehujael. Mehujael became the father of Methushael. Methushael became the father of Lamech. ¹⁹Lamech took two wives: the name of the first one was Adah, and the name of the second one was Zillah. ²⁰Adah gave birth to Jabal, who was the father of those who dwell in tents and have livestock. ²¹His brother's name was Jubal, who was the father of all who handle the harp and pipe. ²²Zillah also gave birth to Tubal Cain, the forger of every cutting instrument of bronze and iron. Tubal Cain's sister was Naamah. ²³Lamech said to his wives, "Adah and Zillah, hear my voice. You wives of Lamech, listen to my speech, for I have slain a man for wounding me, a young man for bruising me. ²⁴If Cain will be avenged seven times, truly Lamech seventy-seven times."

²⁵Adam knew his wife again. She gave birth to a son, and named him Seth, saying, "for God has given me another child instead of Abel, for Cain killed him." ²⁶A son was also born to Seth, and he named him Enosh. At that time men began to call on the LORD's name.

Questions & Discoveries

Respect

Why was Abel and his offering respected by God but not Cain and his offering (Genesis 4:3-5?

"Cain and Abel" is an age-old biblical story that many are familiar with, both believers and non-believers alike. It presents the tale of two brothers, one finding favor with God and the other not so, which ultimately led to the first recorded deceitful and egregious acts of betrayal and slaying of another human. Prior to Cain's deadly act of rage, there's a very interesting account that transpired during their births which influenced Abel and his offering being accepted and

Cain and his offering being rejected by God which fueled Cain's murderous anger. Without any further ado, let's dig into this intriguing account which will serve as the basis for answering the lead question.

First, take notice how Eve presented an inference of joy and excitement during the birth of Cain by blessing him as a gift from God in verse 1. This could be considered normal, after all, because he was her firstborn son after the banning of mankind from the garden of Eden. However, something disturbing happened that can easily be overlooked. When Adam and Eve's first son was born, Eve saw fit to name him "Cain" meaning "to inquire or possess something" in Hebrew. He was also their biological firstborn in and with a sinful nature, never having experienced the godly nature like his parents. To put this plainly, he was born in sin and shaped by iniquity – the jealousy which resided within him. Giving specific attention to his name "Cain," the meaning behind it, and him being born in and with a sinful nature, you can pretty much predict nothing good coming from this person. As a matter of fact, 1 John 3:12 describes him as being the "son of the evil one (being Satan)" which affirms in truth this case concerning him. For Cain, the total makeup of his character resulted in selfishness. Sounds familiar? Remember what caused Eve to first taste of the fruit – lust of the eye, lust of the flesh, and pride of life – her quest for possessing something. Ironically, what caused her to fall was now passed onto their son, Cain, to a stronger degree.

Moving onto the birth of Abel, we don't find that same expression of joy and excitement from Eve as she had with the birth of Cain. Instead, it just briefly mentions his birth and name and transitions forward to their occupations. Nonetheless, here is the background to his name. In Hebrew, the name "Abel" is translated as "Hevel" and means "vapor, breath" which signifies unseen in the natural as something suspended in the air. In other words, Abel was blessed with faith (unseen but present) in God where he recognized and reverenced Him as testified in Hebrews 11:4. Ironically, his character served as the offset of Cain's character. Where Cain was about himself with pretentious reverence toward God, Abel was about remorse and the need of God.

So, why was Abel and his offering respected but not Cain and his offering? In Hebrew, the word "respect" is translated as "shâ'âh" and it means "to consider or compassionate". With both Cain and Abel being born in and with a sinful nature, one (Abel) was about humbly pleasing God, seeking reconciliation for a right standing with Him by faith, which resulted in God having compassion and consideration for him. The other (Cain) was about arrogantly presenting an offering without any genuine remorse or sincerity of reverence toward God. Instead, he chose to operate in his haughty sin nature. Before being judgmental, understand that we still see the same two similar attitudes on display among us today. Those who sincerely repent, humble themselves, and respectfully reverence and seek the need of God by faith, and those who play the role and/or could not care less about God, as illustrated in Luke 18:11-14 (the Pharisee & tax collector). It wasn't so much what was offered to God in terms of fruit or sheep, but what was offered in terms of faith and disbelief/resentment as the reason why Abel and his offering were accepted, and Cain and his offering were rejected.

Sin's Opportunity

How was Cain able to rule over sin by committing sin (Genesis 4:7-8)?

What we read in Genesis 4:7 is very though-provoking. In it we find God's caution presented to Cain being similar to His pronounced revelation upon Eve regarding her "desire" for her husband and the husband "ruling" over her (Genesis 3:16). With Eve, she faced and was overcome with the temptation of being 'like' God as presented by the word of Satan, which led to God causing the consequence of her sin nature being brought forth. However, as we read Genesis 4:6-7 we clearly see that Cain was presented with God's merciful plea as He revealed to him the consequential effects that would occur should he do well or choose not to do well.

⁶"The LORD said to Cain, "Why are you angry? Why has the expression of your face fallen? ⁷If you do well, won't it be lifted

up? If you don't do well, sin crouches at the door. Its desire is for you, but you are to rule over it."

As a refresher from Genesis 3:16 discoveries, we found that the Hebrew word for "desire" is "Teshuqah", meaning "to long after", and the Hebrew word for "rule" to be "Mashal", meaning "to have dominion". Here in Genesis 4:7 we find the exact words being used again. Understand that nothing has changed in the meaning, however the context is quite different. For Eve, the use of "desire" and "rule" were a revelation of what life was to be like for her in the sin nature of the flesh as it relates to the relationship between her and her husband, Adam. However, for Cain "desire" and "rule" would operate simultaneously in the way he was choosing to be – a self-centered, anger-driven possessor (embracer) of his sin nature which blatantly opposed him having a relationship with God.

The sin crouching at his door was that of anger waiting for him to mount it. By Cain embracing the sin of anger, he would then go on to rule (have dominion) over it as it nurtured and shaped his sin nature in every aspect. This resulted in Cain ruling over the sin of anger by embracing it as a lifestyle and as a bold rejection of God's mercy and reverent position. It also provided reason why he heartlessly and so easily committed a homicide (of his biological brother) without any remorse. For him, the power of anger allowed him to be a god and eliminate anyone and/or anything that he feared would compete for glory. He had even gotten to the point of outright disrespecting God with a lie as he flippantly declared not knowing what happened to Abel and sarcastically questioning whether he was his brother's keeper (Genesis 4:9). Furthermore, he was able to rule over sin by accepting and mastering it as a way of life.

Sin's Justice

How was Cain's penalty for sin justly comparable to the sin he committed (Genesis 4:11-12)?

The sin of Cain was a conglomeration of offenses consisting of irreverence towards God, being jealous of Abel and self-entitled, rejecting God and his word, embracing and acting out of anger, committing a homicide, and blatantly lying to God. As we've learned from Genesis 2 and 3, death is the penalty for disobedience as Adam and Eve were made aware by God. Whenever God's will and instructions are foregone, the only available result is there being justice regarding the offense. In order to satisfy the offense, there has to be a price paid. The price must be just in comparison to the offense. So, when Cain decided to ignore God's will and instruction by slaying Abel, he placed himself on trial before God as he figured the consequences were worth him committing the despicable deed. Something he didn't realize was the trick hand of the enemy being opened by God to reveal the costs he (Cain) was now having to pay.

According to Hebrews 11:4, Abel was considered righteous (by his faith in God) and an innocent life lost at the hands of Cain (his older brother). It was unequivocally Cain's decision to walk out of the protected way of righteousness and into the condemned way of sin. In doing so, the offenses he committed against Abel had to be reconciled. By him taking the life of Abel, with Abel's blood soaking the earth, he was found guilty, and his livelihood (as a tiller of the ground) was cursed by the ground no longer producing sustenance by his hands to sustain his life. This represented a life for a life. By Cain pleading ignorant to the crime he committed against Abel, again, he was found guilty and made to be a fugitive and a wanderer. Since Cain was unfit as a brother (and no longer a brother), he was to live as a drifting deserter.

Neither of the sentences were intended as God making Cain's life miserable, instead this was God being just by unveiling to Cain the results of his actions, which were motivated by his gratification in sin, and guided by the enemy. In other words, when sin appears to be more appealing in comparison to righteousness, know that the enemy is only showing what he knows will draw on and appease the flesh and will always downplay the ultimate consequences which he keeps tight-fisted/hidden. It's what happens still today whenever we sin and think we can get away with it. When it comes to light and we have to answer for the offense(s), the light bulb comes on showing the damage we've done and the just price of compensation to be paid.

Did you notice how the crimes he committed against God were not addressed nor configured into God's sentencing? The reasons for this lie in 2 Peter 3:9 as it reads, "The Lord is not slow concerning his promise, as some count slowness; but he is patient with us, not wishing that anyone should perish, but that all should come to repentance." That is to say that when our eternal lives are on the line because of us offending God, he allows us however much time we have remaining on earth to reconcile with Him so that we don't have to suffer the just sentenced of being eternally separated from Him.

Mark of Grace

Why did God mark Cain (a murderer) to protect his life from being taken (Genesis 4:15)?

As we all know, Cain committed what most would consider the most heinous crime by slaying his biological brother out of anger and jealousy of God's acceptance of him (Abel) and his offering. To top it off, he (Cain) wouldn't admit to committing this dastardly deed when asked by God and remorse was never shown. He even brazenly and sarcastically answered God's question with a question – totally disregarding, disrespecting, and challenging God's authority and intelligence. This was a classic case of someone fully embracing the sinful character they had become. As the story goes on, we find that God pronounced sentencing on Cain for his actions surrounding the death of Abel. Get this, still with a rebellious, haughty heart, instead of asking forgiveness and attempting to make things right with God, Cain does something perplexing. Cain had the gall to complain about the burden of his punishment and proceeded to plea with God to spare his life while he's wandering the earth as a fugitive (Genesis 4:13-14). He did this while still taking no ownership for slaying his brother, lying and disrespecting God, and expressing no remorse, yet he sought mercy.

Guess what? We then witness something totally amazing that happens. What is it? It's called God being merciful. God owes no one anything, yet He saw fit to restrain taking harsher action (of physical death) upon Cain. Not only did he allow him to live as a fugitive and wanderer, but He also listened and honored the plea of

Cain by appointing a sign for Cain that prohibited anyone from slaying him. As a matter of fact, God went a step further and told Cain that anyone who slays him, that He will dole out seven times greater vengeance to that person on Cain's behalf (Genesis 4:15). If you get nothing else, get this point. God is truly merciful. Psalm 103:8 states it this way, "The LORD is merciful and gracious, slow to anger, and abundant in lovingkindness." He loves his creation to the utmost and wills that repentance is sought for reconciliation by each person. This is one of the reasons why He's able to extend mercy to those who embrace sin but still have enough sense to ask for mercy from Him. It's not that it's unfair, it's that He's God and He's a just God. It's in His mercy that time is permitted for sinners to repent because He does not will for anyone to physically and spiritually die in their sin and then have to join in with the punishment that was made for Satan and his followers. An example of this can be seen in how Pharaoh was given multiple times to repent and do what was right, but instead he chose to continually decline, which eventually led to the horrible death of his army in the Red Sea (Exodus, chapters 7-14).

God's mercy is never intended for anyone to take for granted, but for repentance. It's not showing Him as weak, but quite the opposite – it exemplifies the length, depth, and strength of His love for us beyond all measure (Romans 8:35-39). Although Cain committed an egregious act, God still loved him, protected him and provided him opportunity for repenting and obtaining a right relationship with Him. It's much like Jesus did on the cross while He was facing ridicule and shame. Instead of condemning them, He said, "Father, forgive them, for they know not what they are doing" (Luke 23:34). God knows when we're operating out of a character that is brought on by existing and inherited sin natures. However, He never changes, never stop loving, and always willing to extend mercy to bring us back to reality and relationship with Him. This is exactly what He was doing with Cain.

His Own God

What is the significance of Lamech proclaiming vengeance of his own volition (Genesis 4:24)?

Before we get into discussing Lamech, let's take a moment to examine the magnitude of Cain's punishment. When he rejected God's authority, he severed his relationship with God as brought about by his own doing and will. This does not mean he became an atheist or an agnostic. He believed and knew who God was, but he rejected His authority over his life. Once that relationship was severed, because of his rebellious nature, he received the punishment of being driven from the whereabouts of Adam and Eve into the land of Nod (which in Hebrew means wandering or vagrancy). As previously discussed, he totally embraced his sinful nature and was fine with his decision (as indicated by him failing to show any remorse or repentance). He was now at a place in his life where he could be his own god and live without godly restraints and guidance. Sadly, the results of his sinful nature exacerbated astronomically as it affected and passed on throughout his lineage. In Exodus 34:6-7, we find that (without forgiveness) the results of sins are generationally passed on:

> "The LORD passed by before him, and proclaimed, 'The LORD! The LORD, a merciful and gracious God, slow to anger, and abundant in lovingkindness and truth, keeping lovingkindness for thousands, forgiving iniquity and disobedience and sin; and who will by no means clear the guilty, visiting the iniquity of the fathers on the children, and on the children's children, on the third and on the fourth generation.'"

So, here we are a few generations in and it's when we find the sinful nature of Lamech exhibited in a god-like manner as inherited from his great-great-great-grandfather, Cain. In Hebrew the name "Lamech" means "one who is strong and powerful." Using his natural strength as a show of power, he decided to take for himself two wives. To further bolster his ego, he goes on to conceitedly stand before his wives as a god to announce his crime of slaying someone and proclaiming to be avenged seventy-seven times if any harm come upon him. Remember, vengeance is God's to proclaim and execute (Genesis 4:15 / Deuteronomy 32:35)); however, Lamech decides to act as if he is a god, and disrespectfully and pridefully mimics God's authority. Furthermore, just like Cain, he saw no wrong in his merciless actions, and expected not only mercy but retribution as well for anyone bringing any harm upon him. The significance of Lamech proclaiming vengeance of his own volition is that he perceived himself to be his own god not only by the natural strength and power he possessed but also his ability to appear intimidating and live as such.

From the roots of any type of sin, greater sin is produced (when not addressed and left to fester). Sure, it is easy for anyone to point the finger and think or say something like, "How in the world could such a person sleep at night with a good conscious?" The truth is, such a person's conscious has been seared (numbed / desensitized) to their sinful nature which makes whatever they do seemingly right in their own eyes (1 Timothy 4:1-3). The nature of Lamech lives on today in many choosing to not have God as part of their lives and instead irreverently capitalizing on taking for themselves and misusing the principles and authoritative words of God.

Two Different Worlds

What is the significance of Cain and Enoch in contrast to Seth and Enosh (Genesis 4:17 / Genesis 4:26?

Upon being expelled from the whereabouts near Adam and Eve, in Genesis 4:17 it is revealed that Cain had relations with his wife, leading to them having a son called Enoch. In Hebrew, the name Enoch is translated as "Ḥănōk" and means "to train, initiate, dedicate, or inaugurate". In the same verse, we read that Cain built a city and named it after Enoch. The representation of Cain building and naming this city after Enoch was a dedication to usher in whatever work of the flesh he (Cain) deemed as glory not only unto himself but other generations that came and followed after his ways. It was for nothing short of self-vindication of the 'respect' he failed to receive from God (because of his choice to embrace and act in anger) that he decided to be his own god and arrogantly build what would seemingly bring glory and respect to him and his lineage.

In Genesis 4:25-26, it is disclosed that Eve gives birth to another son, named Seth. In Hebrew the name Seth is translated as 'Sheth' and means 'appointed or placed; substitute'. This name rightly fits him as Eve stated he was a replacement of the slain Abel. In time, Seth eventually had a son born to him who was given the name Enosh, and is translated as 'Ĕnōš in Hebrew and means "mankind; man". In other words, it was a resetting of the stage representing what was in the beginning when God created Adam (which means 'mankind') and there was a harmonious relationship which existed between them. Interestingly in verse 26, we're told that Enosh's birth marked a time when men began to call on the LORD's name. What this proclamation signifies is the beginning of prayer in seeking and calling upon God as opposed to hiding from him (as Adam and Eve had done). It was an avenue for rebuilding relationship between man and God.

The significance of Cain and Enoch in contrast to Seth and Enosh centered on what was being built. On the one hand, there was building for man's self-glorification; and on the other, there was building for man's relationship with God. Cain was producing a lineage based on doing works for temporal self-satisfaction and appeasement without restraints whereas Seth was instead producing a lineage of God seekers who would pray, trust and depend on God and His word for eternal life. This brings to light the same contrast between true believers and those who promote "the power of I" mentality. One group is exercising faith in God through prayer and supplication (according to Philippians 4:6) and the other group is all about selfish ambitions (Romans 2:5-9).

GENESIS 5

Overview

This chapter opens by briefly recounting the creation to the physical death of Adam. Afterward it proceeds in providing the lineage following Seth and treks nine generations to the births of Shem, Ham, and Japheth (Noah's sons). Interestingly, all we know of Cain's lineage was summed up in the preceding chapter, which is strongly indicative of God wanting us to know and concentrate on the lineage of Seth, from which we come. This chapter may appear sort of mundane when reading it at face value. After all, it looks to be just a genealogy listing of unpronounceable, gibberish names. However, the meaning of those names defines mankind's various individual purposes in establishing and passing along the common connection of faith in God. It's equivalent to what we find in 1 Corinthians 12:12-31, in there being many members with different functions, but all being one body. Lastly, we read of Lamech pronouncing a prophecy upon the birth and naming of his son, Noah. In this chapter, we'll discuss and examine the following discoveries:

1. What is the likeness and image of Adam in which Seth was born?
2. What distinguished Enoch so that God took him?

3. What did Lamech's prophecy reveal?

Scriptural Reading

¹This is the book of the generations of Adam. In the day that God created man, he made him in God's likeness. ²He created them male and female and blessed them. On the day they were created, he named them Adam. ³Adam lived one hundred thirty years and became the father of a son in his own likeness, after his image, and named him Seth.⁴The days of Adam after he became the father of Seth were eight hundred years, and he became the father of other sons and daughters. ⁵All the days that Adam lived were nine hundred thirty years, then he died. ⁶Seth lived one hundred five years, then became the father of Enosh. ⁷Seth lived after he became the father of Enosh eight hundred seven years and became the father of other sons and daughters. ⁸All of the days of Seth were nine hundred twelve years, then he died. ⁹Enosh lived ninety years and became the father of Kenan. ¹⁰Enosh lived after he became the father of Kenan eight hundred fifteen years and became the father of other sons and daughters. ¹¹All of the days of Enosh were nine hundred five years, then he died. ¹²Kenan lived seventy years, then became the father of Mahalalel. ¹³Kenan lived after he became the father of Mahalalel eight hundred forty years and became the father of other sons and daughters ¹⁴and all of the days of Kenan were nine hundred ten years, then he died. ¹⁵Mahalalel lived sixty-five years, then became the father of Jared. ¹⁶Mahalalel lived after he became the father of Jared eight hundred thirty years and became the father of other sons and daughters. ¹⁷All of the days of Mahalalel were eight hundred ninety-five years, then he died. ¹⁸Jared lived one hundred sixty-two years, then became the father of Enoch. ¹⁹Jared lived after he became the father of Enoch eight hundred years and became the father of other sons

and daughters. [20]All of the days of Jared were nine hundred sixty-two years, then he died.

[21]Enoch lived sixty-five years, then became the father of Methuselah. [22]After Methuselah's birth, Enoch walked with God for three hundred years, and became the father of more sons and daughters. [23]All the days of Enoch were three hundred sixty-five years. [24]Enoch walked with God, and he was not found, for God took him.

[25]Methuselah lived one hundred eighty-seven years, then became the father of Lamech. [26]Methuselah lived after he became the father of Lamech seven hundred eighty-two years and became the father of other sons and daughters. [27]All the days of Methuselah were nine hundred sixty-nine years, then he died.

[28]Lamech lived one hundred eighty-two years, then became the father of a son. [29]He named him Noah, saying, "This one will comfort us in our work and in the toil of our hands, caused by the ground which the LORD has cursed." [30]Lamech lived after he became the father of Noah five hundred ninety-five years, and became the father of other sons and daughters. [31]All the days of Lamech were seven hundred seventy-seven years, then he died.

[32]Noah was five hundred years old, then Noah became the father of Shem, Ham, and Japheth.

Questions & Discoveries

Another Image

What is the likeness and image of Adam in which Seth was born (Genesis 5:3)?

Going back to Genesis 1 in this publication, we read and examined the meaning behind God creating mankind in His image (Genesis 1:26-28). The core of being created in His image is mankind possessing godly intelligence, expression, and influence. These identified entities were and are essential for us fostering relationships with Him as God and among mankind in general. Also, they are crucial in fulfilling our purpose. Then in Chapter 3, we read and examined the sin nature that mankind was birthed into by way of disobedience to God's instruction which forbade eating from the tree of the knowledge of good and evil. Once that sin nature came alive within mankind, a new likeness and image began morphing away from godliness and toward sinful thinking, expressing, and corrupt speech and behaviors. In doing so, mankind was and has become, slowly but surely, desensitized and rebellious to the word and authority of God as exemplified by the character of Cain.

That leads us to Genesis 5:3, where it shares of Adam becoming father to another son (Seth) who was born according to Adam's own likeness and image. What this implies is Seth simultaneously possessing 1) the spiritual likeness and image of Adam in faith, which connects him to God; and 2) the physical and spiritual likeness and image of Adam's sin nature, which represents his contention with sin in the flesh. Although Adam still possessed a somewhat fractured spiritual connection to God which enabled him to maintain a relationship with God, he was now having to contend with the sinful nature of his new image in the natural state (lust of the eye, lust of the flesh, and pride of life).

The very likeness and image that Adam incurred was transferred to his son (Seth), who not only was a substitute of Abel but an appointed one to carry on the faith in God (totally opposite from the route Cain had chosen). Seth possessing the likeness and image of Adam was a burden to bear and continues through the lineage of believers today. That is until Jesus came on the scene as the last Adam, replacing and performing what the first Adam failed and could not do (1 Corinthians 15:45) in reconciling us to God. When we accept Jesus as Lord and Savior, we become reconciled to right relationships with God because of Jesus becoming and defeating sin on our behalf (2 Corinthians 5:21).

Something worth noting is that the beginning of this chapter skipped over Cain, who was the first born of Adam and Eve, and went directly to the birth of Seth. Let this be a testimony of God honoring and having delight in those whose faith is steadfast in Him. Psalm 149:4 proclaims, "For the LORD takes pleasure in his people. He crowns the humble with salvation." Spend time nurturing a sincere and reverent relationship with Him and passing on the faith to those coming after you.

Taken Away

What distinguished Enoch so that God took him (Genesis 5:22-24)?

In Genesis 5, when reading the genealogy from Seth to Noah, it can be visibly noted that each of the patriarchs followed the order of being born, having a son, living more years, having other sons and daughters, and then dying. That is except for one, being Enoch. Unlike the other patriarchs, we're given a bit more information that differentiated Enoch's relationship with God compared to the others. As previously discovered, Seth was the substitute for Abel. As Abel's appointed replacement, he inherited the responsibility of continuing in the order of Abel by recognizing the need for and seeking reconciliation with God (Genesis 4:4). In doing so, he was able to train and pass on the faith and ritual to those coming after him, beginning with his son, Enosh, who instituted prayer and worship.

By the meaning of their names (indicated in brackets), it is safe to assume the patriarchs Enosh [man], Kenan [acquire], Mahalalel [praise of God], and Jared [descent] all followed suit by accepting, respecting, and living lifestyles honoring God. However, when Enoch arrives on the scene and before and after the birth of his son Methuselah [to die, to send forth] something dissimilar occurs apart from the other patriarchs. Let's delve in by starting with his name. In Hebrew the name 'Enoch' is translated as "Ḥănōk" and means "to train, initiate, dedicate, or inaugurate." His name was prophetic in that it signified his dedicated closeness and commitment to God, which was exemplified by his walking with God all his days before and after the birth of Methuselah (Genesis 5:22-24). The walk God shared with mankind was an agreeable walk (as Amos 3:3 speaks of), meaning they were in sync: God's goodness and blessings laid upon mankind and mankind's reverence and honor presented to God. His walk with God was not only agreeable, but very valuable. It was so valuable that God took him alive to be with Him (Genesis 5:24).

Many may wonder, "What makes Enoch's relationship with God any different or of more value than the others?" Let's go back to Genesis 3:8 where the word "walking" is first mentioned in relation to God and Adam and Eve. Prior to the fall of mankind, they shared a peaceful bond and relationship with God to where God would meet them, and they would openly share in conversations. Why describe their bond and relationship as peaceful? Because there was a peace between God and mankind with nothing hindering their relationship until sin entered on the scene, which disturbed the peace between them by crippling man's ability to walk agreeably with God. That peaceful relationship and agreeable walk that once existed between God and mankind was never based on nor intended to be based on one-sidedness. It was a reciprocal appreciation among all parties, which is what made the relationship significantly valuable. Think about it for a moment; God was able to freely relate, communicate, and shower his blessings and goodness upon mankind who were created in His image – designed as being comparable with God. However, when sin entered, it awakened the desires of mankind to seek what benefits self, and this initiated a relationship based on lusts and pride, quite the polar opposite of God's character.

As Enoch comes on the scene, his relationship with God is taken to a level of having reestablished peace and an agreeable walk as he is submerged in God's righteousness. Enoch's distinguished lifestyle and spiritual connection to God was refreshing for God and served as righteousness with God. What Enoch offered was a loyal lifestyle consisting of him acting justly, loving mercy, and walking humbly with God as identified in Micah 6:8, which allowed for him to be acceptable in the sight of God. He did not allow prayer and worship to be a religious duty, they were a conviction in his heart and a dedication to the God he knows, loves, and fully embraces. Just as Enoch was taken up by God, so will those of us who are alive during the return of Jesus according to 1 Thessalonians 4:16-17.

Living up to the Name

What did Lamech's prophecy reveal (Genesis 5:29)?

In Genesis 5:28-29, we are introduced to the birth of Lamech's son, Noah. Many of us are familiar with Noah from either early Sunday school stories and songs about the ark or pulpit sermons surrounding him being used by God to build an ark, something seemingly impossible yet extraordinarily amazing and unheard of (especially during his era without modernized resources). In Hebrew the name Noah is translated as "Noach" and means "rest." When he was born and upon giving him the name Noah, Lamech pronounced a prophecy concerning him. The prophecy was "This one will comfort us in our work and in the toil of our hands, caused by the ground which the Lord has cursed." So, what is it that Lamech was actually revealing in this prophetic message? One general interpretation could be that Noah was appointed as the one who would somehow come up with a new idea or way of doing work and/or how often it was done, with an implication of offering comfort and being less burdensome on their hands and bodies. After all, they did not have the machinery and advanced technologies we have nowadays. During their era, work was very arduous and tough. Without having OSHA standards and requirements like we do today, it's a guarantee their working environments led to massive high-risk injuries and deaths as well as making for long days and many restless nights. Therefore, this could easily have been what Lamech was referring to in his naming of Noah. He was seeking relief from what they were experiencing in work conditions.

It is always interesting how God works in certain situations. There are times we find ourselves praying for something that benefits us, but God uses that prayer for benefitting someone else or others outside of our generation. Such is the case with Lamech's prophecy over Noah. Lamech's short-sightedness had him seeking relief for the work life they were contending with. Like Lamech, it's within our awakened sinful nature that we seek relief from its consequences, and we all know it all too well. However, for God, He sees the bigger picture and far ahead of just comforting what affects us today. He stands ready to provide greater, more far-reaching mercy that reaches many more than just the circle we know and are part of. Does that make the prophetic message pronounced over Noah null and void? Certainly not.

Lamech's prophetic message was directly in line with what God was readying to manifest many years later in Noah's life. It would usher in the answer and comfort of mankind from their work and the toil of their hands in a very unconventional way, and because of the massive spread of sin. It wasn't the work related to the cursed ground they were needing rest from; it was the sinful nature and normalcy of it that mankind and the ground needed rest from, as identified in Genesis 6. God knows the way to deal with mankind's sin, He knows how and when to reset, and He knows whom to use. The revelation of Lamech's prophecy would come to pass in the form of Noah's ark and the flooding of the world at the cost of all but 8 lives. Because of his faith and righteousness in the sight of God, Noah (and his family) received rest from the prevailing wicked works and hands of the wicked.

GENESIS 6

Overview

The sinful nature of man and God's response form the center of attention for this chapter. It picks up where mankind has rapidly multiplied throughout the earth, and quickly delves into the illegitimate marriages between the godly men from the lineage of Seth and the ungodly women from the lineage of Cain. It was through these unsanctioned marriages that sin compounded, affecting all facets of life, which resulted in God having mindful regrets and a grieving heart. Yet, because of His lovingkindness and enduring mercy, He was just in His decision to destroy all mankind with the exception of Noah, his wife, his three sons, and their wives. God used Noah as the saving grace for building the ark and preserving a new lineage of mankind to come because Noah was declared a righteous man who walked with God. As we read this chapter regarding the end of the Adamic era, we'll discuss and examine the following discoveries:

1. What is the distinction between the sons of God and the daughters of men?
2. What is the significance of God limiting the days of mankind to 120 years?

3. Why didn't God take Noah just as he had taken Enoch?

Scriptural Reading

[1]When men began to multiply on the surface of the ground, and daughters were born to them, [2]God's sons saw that men's daughters were beautiful, and they took any that they wanted for themselves as wives. [3]The LORD said, "My Spirit will not strive with man forever, because he also is flesh; so his days will be one hundred twenty years." [4]The Nephilim were in the earth in those days, and also after that, when God's sons came in to men's daughters and had children with them. Those were the mighty men who were of old, men of renown.
[5]The LORD saw that the wickedness of man was great in the earth, and that every imagination of the thoughts of man's heart was continually only evil. [6]The LORD was sorry that he had made man on the earth, and it grieved him in his heart. [7]The LORD said, "I will destroy man whom I have created from the surface of the ground—man, along with animals, creeping things, and birds of the sky—for I am sorry that I have made them." [8]But Noah found favor in the LORD's eyes.
[9]This is the history of the generations of Noah: Noah was a righteous man, blameless among the people of his time. Noah walked with God. [10]Noah became the father of three sons: Shem, Ham, and Japheth. [11]The earth was corrupt before God, and the earth was filled with violence. [12]God saw the earth, and saw that it was corrupt, for all flesh had corrupted their way on the earth.
[13]God said to Noah, "I will bring an end to all flesh, for the earth is filled with violence through them. Behold, I will destroy them and the earth. [14]Make a ship of gopher wood. You shall make rooms in the ship and shall seal it inside and outside with pitch.[15]This is how you shall make it. The length of the ship shall be three hundred cubits, its width fifty cubits, and its height thirty cubits. [16]You shall make a roof in the ship, and you shall finish it to a cubit upward. You shall set the door of the ship in its side. You shall make it with lower, second, and third

levels. ¹⁷I, even I, will bring the flood of waters on this earth, to destroy all flesh having the breath of life from under the sky. Everything that is in the earth will die. ¹⁸But I will establish my covenant with you. You shall come into the ship, you, your sons, your wife, and your sons' wives with you. ¹⁹Of every living thing of all flesh, you shall bring two of every sort into the ship, to keep them alive with you. They shall be male and female. ²⁰Of the birds after their kind, of the livestock after their kind, of every creeping thing of the ground after its kind, two of every sort will come to you, to keep them alive. ²¹Take with you some of all food that is eaten and gather it to yourself; and it will be for food for you, and for them." ²²Thus Noah did. He did all that God commanded him.

Questions & Discoveries

Godly Men Meeting Male Men

What is the distinction between the sons of God and the daughters of men (Genesis 6:1-2, 4)?

The sons of God are in reference to the lineage of Seth, whereas the daughters of men are in reference to the lineage of Cain. How is this statement confirmed? Take another look at verse one. It states that 'men began to multiply.' What men are referred to here? All men in general, being those of the lineage of Seth and those of the lineage of Cain. The lineage of Seth are counted as the sons of God as identified in Genesis 5. They carried on a knowledge of, reliance on, and walk with God -a relationship- which is identified by each of the patriarch's names. That is quite the opposite for the descendants of Cain. They had no room for, no recognition of, and no reverence toward God as they embraced their sinful nature by realizing self-value in works, free-spirit, mind and emotions, and material things as discussed in Genesis 4.

During the days leading up to the ark being constructed, the descendants of Cain's great-great-great-grandson (Lamech) existed. Genesis 6:5 exposes the wickedness of man having been great throughout the earth and their minds and hearts were continually evil. Ironically, in reference to their declined and infectious morals which became widespread, the names of Lamech's children reveal and coincide with the major influences directly taking place prior to and during the building of the ark:

Jabal represented those leading wandering lives (those without purpose)
Jubal represented those who were entranced by and danced to the beat of their own music (those without boundaries)
Tubal-Cain represented those who built what exemplified themselves (those who were idol worshippers)
Naamah represented women of beauty (those who were seductresses)

In Genesis 6:4, we're introduced to the term "Nephilim" for the first time in scripture (also found in Numbers 13:31-33). It means "giants" or "the fallen ones". They came on the scene in the days directly prior to the building of the ark and were the offspring from the intermingling of the sons of God with the daughters of men. Their nature took sin to another level of full-blown wickedness and evil akin to blasphemous behavior. Before judging, think about how this same attitude is widely spread and lives among us today. It's represented by people who profess to believe in God but whose lifestyle and speech is contradictory. On a side note, Noah's wife, though nameless in scripture, is believed to be Naamah (Lamech's daughter) according to some apocryphal literature. This would explain why it is mentioned in Genesis 6:4 that the Nephilim were in the earth during those days (not before) and also after (as depicted in Numbers 13:33). What makes the Nephilim appear as giants could not only pertain to their physical stature but also to their selfish intellectual convictions, which also solidifies them being in a fallen state.

The Countdown

What is the significance of God limiting the days of mankind to 120 years (Genesis 6:3)?

The statement made by God and recorded in Genesis 6:3 has been erroneously viewed by many as God limiting mankind's years of age to a maximum of 120 years. Although a seemingly acceptable intellectual guess, it is out of context to that to which God was referring. Let's look at Genesis 6:1-3:

> ¹When men began to multiply on the surface of the ground, and daughters were born to them, ²God's sons saw that men's daughters were beautiful, and they took any that they wanted for themselves as wives. ³The LORD said, "My Spirit will not strive with man forever, because he also is flesh; so, his days will be one hundred twenty years."

What we find first is there being a huge problem developing in which the sons of God (those who were in relationship with God) began intermingling by marriage with the daughters of men (those who were considered infidels). This mixing was straining and strangling the sons of God's relationships with Him – pushing God out as the sinful nature and ways of Cain were starting to prevail as an acceptable lifestyle. Because of the prevailing influence of sin becoming the norm, God justly decided to deal with those sins by purging those who were affected by sin and sinfully affecting others. Secondly, He set in place and allowed a grace period of 120 years (three generations of time), the same amount of time it would take Noah to complete the ark. It was during that grace period that Noah walked obediently with God while serving as His witness to those caught up in the shenanigans of sin. By Him declaring His Spirit not striving (abiding) with man forever, He was issuing a countdown warning to those walking in the flesh. They were given 120 years of opportunity to repent, return to Him, witness the testimony of His goodness through the life of Noah, and to train their children better by telling them about God. Instead, they chose not to because life in the world meant more than having a relationship with Him. The irresponsible decision of the elders not only brought judgment on them but their children and their children's children, too – all following in the way of what seemed right in their own eyes (Proverbs 21:2).

Lastly, this situation shines light on the seriousness of the consequences of sin and how a little leaven leavens the entire lump (Galatians 5:9). In other words, the very speech and actions we mimic and adapt from the world affects those in our world. They also have dire consequences that are not only limited to the offender, but those connected to the offender as well. Every day we are alive is an opportunity for us to be mindful of who we are (as His children), to be a witness of who He is, and live a testimony of hope. In essence, God is using us to build an A.R.K. of our own to save others by us living ACCEPTABLE to Him, RELAYING the message of hope and salvation in Christ, and KEEPING ourselves and other believing brothers and sisters focused on the mission.

Making Way for a Greater Salvation to Come

Why didn't God take Noah just as He had taken Enoch (Genesis 5:22-24 & Genesis 6:9-22)?

God loves us! What a sure word to know and accept as truth! This is spoken with the fact of knowing He is preparing and waiting to take us one day as well. It's interesting to think about Enoch being taken after he walked with God for 300 years (Genesis 5:22), and Noah was estimated to be around 480 years old when he was identified as being righteous and blameless among the people and walking with God (Genesis 6:9), yet he was left to build an ark for he and his family. It may seem a bit unfair, but it wasn't, and neither is God unfair – He is just! He had a purpose for Enoch just as He had a purpose for Noah, and just as He has a purpose for us.

In Genesis 6:18, there's a profound statement God makes to Noah. He tells him, "I will establish my covenant with you." What does that mean? It means Noah (like each of us as believers) is a conduit of God's mercy and grace covenant. Noah's job was to build the ark, but his purpose was to carry on the message as a living witness. God never created mankind to destroy mankind nor to live in the prison of sin. Noah building the ark is akin to us today building our faith – it's what sustains us and serves as a prayer rope of salvation for others. Noah building the ark wasn't only about him and his family; it was for all of mankind who would come after the flood. It was for readying the scene for Christ's arrival approximately 2,000 years later. Every calculation of God consisted of His mercy, grace, and lovingkindness for us, and with us in mind. In His calculation, Noah being the last righteous and blameless man standing was just the seed God needed to plant in an ark. He would then use water to lift the ark as a tool of salvation for the greater purpose of mankind repopulating the earth and reestablishing the foundation of faith. In doing so, that event allowed for God's Spirit to continue abiding with mankind. In a nutshell, Enoch was taken for the purpose God has for him in the future (Revelation 11:1-14) and Noah remained for the purpose of creating a future (Genesis 8:17).

GENESIS 7

Overview

The allegiance of Noah to God versus the allegiance of the people to sin leads to the consequential judgement within this chapter. In this chapter, we are introduced to God being longsuffering and merciful, Noah being righteous and blameless, the people being sinful and rebellious, and God's plan of grace shown towards Noah and his family. God is preparing for a reset with mankind and has chosen Noah, based on his righteousness, to anchor His plan. Noah is given specific instructions by God to build an ark, something never heard of nor thought of before. God fills Noah in on His plan to flood the earth as a just result of mankind's prevailing sins, killing everything that had the breath of life except what and who He instructs Noah to bring into the ark. In reading this chapter, there were a few pondering questions that arose to be discussed and examined:

1. How was Noah's righteousness seen by God?
2. Why were Noah and his family in the ark seven days prior to the start of the floodwaters?
3. Could 40 days of nonstop dispersed water really flood the earth?

Scriptural Reading

[1]The LORD said to Noah, "Come with all of your household into the ship, for I have seen your righteousness before me in this generation. [2]You shall take seven pairs of every clean animal with you, the male and his female. Of the animals that are not clean, take two, the male and his female. [3]Also of the birds of the sky, seven and seven, male and female, to keep seed alive on the surface of all the earth. [4]In seven days, I will cause it to rain on the earth for forty days and forty nights. I will destroy every living thing that I have made from the surface of the ground."

[5]Noah did everything that the LORD commanded him.

[6]Noah was six hundred years old when the flood of waters came on the earth. [7]Noah went into the ship with his sons, his wife, and his sons' wives, because of the floodwaters. [8]Clean animals, unclean animals, birds, and everything that creeps on the ground [9]went by pairs to Noah into the ship, male and female, as God commanded Noah. [10]After the seven days, the floodwaters came on the earth. [11]In the six hundredth year of Noah's life, in the second month, on the seventeenth day of the month, on that day all the fountains of the great deep burst open, and the sky's windows opened. [12]It rained on the earth forty days and forty nights.

[13]In the same day Noah, and Shem, Ham, and Japheth—the sons of Noah—and Noah's wife and the three wives of his sons with them, entered into the ship— [14]they, and every animal after its kind, all the livestock after their kind, every creeping thing that creeps on the earth after its kind, and every bird after its kind, every bird of every sort. [15]Pairs from all flesh with the breath of life in them went into the ship to Noah. [16]Those who went in, went in male and female of all flesh, as God commanded him; then the LORD shut him in. [17]The flood was forty days on the earth. The waters increased, and lifted up the ship, and it was lifted up above the earth. [18]The waters rose, and increased greatly on the earth; and the ship floated on the surface of the waters. [19]The waters rose very high on the earth.

All the high mountains that were under the whole sky were covered. [20]The waters rose fifteen cubits higher, and the mountains were covered. [21]All flesh died that moved on the earth, including birds, livestock, animals, every creeping thing that creeps on the earth, and every man. [22]All on the dry land, in whose nostrils was the breath of the spirit of life, died. [23]Every living thing was destroyed that was on the surface of the ground, including man, livestock, creeping things, and birds of the sky. They were destroyed from the earth. Only Noah was left, and those who were with him in the ship. [24]The waters flooded the earth one hundred fifty days.

Questions & Discoveries

Good and Faithful Servant

How was Noah's righteousness seen by God (Genesis 7:1)?

Here in Genesis 7:1, we read the words of God welcoming Noah into the ark based on Him seeing Noah's righteousness. The question that many of us may ponder is, "What righteousness did Noah display?" After all, as many of us have read and know, Isaiah 64:6 declares that all our righteousness are like a polluted garment. And again, Ephesians 2:8-9 tells us "…for by grace you have been saved through faith, and that not of yourselves; it is the gift of God, not of works, that no one should boast." So, what is the righteousness Noah displayed that God saw?

Think back to Genesis 4:4 when God found Abel and his offering acceptable and then in Genesis 6:9 where we read and learned that Noah was considered as a righteous man who was blameless among the people and walked with God. The righteousness that God observed in Abel and Noah is the same righteousness He saw in the early lineage of Seth from the days of Enosh to Enoch and now Noah. That righteousness was a heart of repentance, a humble spirit, and a reverence for the one true God. The testimonial byproduct was in Noah's unwavering loyalty to God, knowing He needed God, unlike those in his day who rejected God.

His need of God resulted in him possessing courage, integrity, and commitment. He had the courage to trust and walk with God despite the so-called fun and temporal prosperity that everyone else was experiencing. He had integrity in being mindful of who he was and who God is. He was committed to being a living testimony for those coming after him.

With all of that being the case, the greatest righteousness that God saw in Noah was the birth of Jesus some 2,000 years in the future. Jesus would be the righteousness for the sake of all mankind that has ever lived. As a matter of fact, 1 Corinthians 1:30 states, "Because of Him, you are in Christ Jesus, who was made to us wisdom from God, and righteousness and sanctification, and redemption…" When we surrender, accept, and walk with God, He becomes the change in us by way of His Spirit. That change identifies us in the righteousness of Jesus, which makes us acceptable before God. When God invited Noah and his family into the ark, it served as a foretelling of Him inviting us, as good and faithful servants, into His joy as stated by Jesus in His illustration in Matthew 25:23.

Grace Period

Why was Noah and his family in the ark seven days prior to the start of the floodwaters (Genesis 7:7-10)?

Unlike mankind, God isn't quick to dismiss and discard us. The mercy He shows is filled with His love towards all mankind and the prayers of Jesus and believers on mankind's behalf. In 2 Peter 3:9, He is described as being longsuffering toward us, willing that none should perish, but that all repent. God's intent for creating mankind was never for destroying but for relationship. Although relationship is at the heart of God, He's not going to make us choose Him. It's by our own free will in accepting Him that we're able to be in relationship with Him.

All of that was said to point out the fact of His steadfast, enduring mercy even in the quiet midst of warnings. He had Noah and his family come into the ark seven days prior to the floodwaters

(Genesis 7:10)– that was an invitation of mercy for those on the outside to repent. He had Moses go to Pharoah 10 times to free the Hebrews (Exodus 7-14) – that was an invitation of mercy for Pharoah and his army to let His people go in peace. He had Joshua and the Hebrew army to march around the wall of Jericho seven days (Joshua 6) – that was an invitation of mercy for those within the walls of Jericho to surrender. Whether it's seven, 10, or however long, those examples along with many others throughout the scripture are proof of His mercy and love for us. God's grace period nourishes and births the fruit of the Spirit in those who are saved but serves as a lifeline for those needing to be saved.

The Floodwaters

Could 40 days of nonstop dispersed water really flood the earth (Genesis 7:11 & 17-20)?

God Himself said to Abraham in Genesis 18:14, "Is there anything too hard for the LORD?" Amazingly, after asking the question, what God promised Abraham eventually came to pass. So, the lead question regarding the floodwaters in Genesis 7 is not without a sufficient answer. Genesis 7:11 tells us of two locations from which the water came causing the flood: the fountains/springs of the deep (on earth), and the clouds of the sky. Guess what? Until then, the earth had never experienced rain according to Genesis 2:5 and 6, which means the clouds had been forming and preparing to disperse hundreds of years of rainwater all within a 40-day period, and the fountains/springs of the deep had been storing and readying to release the pressure of water by way of geysers. With it all occurring simultaneously, the answer is a resounding "Yes, 40 days of nonstop dispersed water can and did flood the earth as described in Genesis 7:17-20!" Sadly, because of the people never seeing/experiencing rain, instead of inquiring of Noah how to get their lives right with God, they chose to mock him to their own demise.

GENESIS 8

Overview

Although it wasn't revealed within the scriptures how life must have been for Noah and his family being confined in the ark, their blessing was in the favor of God using the ark to preserve their lives. This chapter provides details regarding the length and receding of the floodwaters, Noah seeking a sign of dry land, God speaking to Noah, and God's established covenant with Himself. The following discoveries will be discussed and examined:

1. What is meant by "God remembered Noah…"?
2. Why did Noah send out a raven?
3. What was the significance of God not speaking to Noah until it was time for him and his family to depart the ark?
4. Why would burnt offerings please and motivate God to establish a covenant with Himself?

Scriptural Reading

[1]God remembered Noah, all the animals, and all the livestock that were with him in the ship; and God made a wind to pass over the earth. The waters subsided. [2]The deep's fountains and

the sky's windows were also stopped, and the rain from the sky was restrained. [3]The waters continually receded from the earth. After the end of one hundred fifty days the waters receded. [4]The ship rested in the seventh month, on the seventeenth day of the month, on Ararat's mountains. [5]The waters receded continually until the tenth month. In the tenth month, on the first day of the month, the tops of the mountains were visible.

[6]At the end of forty days, Noah opened the window of the ship which he had made, [7]and he sent out a raven. It went back and forth, until the waters were dried up from the earth. [8]He himself sent out a dove to see if the waters were abated from the surface of the ground, [9]but the dove found no place to rest her foot, and she returned into the ship to him, for the waters were on the surface of the whole earth. He put out his hand, and took her, and brought her to him into the ship. [10]He waited yet another seven days; and again, he sent the dove out of the ship. [11]The dove came back to him at evening and behold, in her mouth was a freshly plucked olive leaf. So, Noah knew that the waters were abated from the earth. [12]He waited yet another seven days and sent out the dove; and she didn't return to him anymore.

[13]In the six hundred first year, in the first month, the first day of the month, the waters were dried up from the earth. Noah removed the covering of the ship and looked. He saw that the surface of the ground was dry. [14]In the second month, on the twenty-seventh day of the month, the earth was dry.

[15]God spoke to Noah, saying, [16]"Go out of the ship, you, your wife, your sons, and your sons' wives with you. [17]Bring out with you every living thing that is with you of all flesh, including birds, livestock, and every creeping thing that creeps on the earth, that they may breed abundantly in the earth, and be fruitful, and multiply on the earth."

[18]Noah went out, with his sons, his wife, and his sons' wives with him. [19]Every animal, every creeping thing, and every bird, whatever moves on the earth, after their families, went out of the ship.

[20]Noah built an altar to the LORD, and took of every clean animal, and of every clean bird, and offered burnt offerings on

the altar. [21]The LORD smelled the pleasant aroma. The LORD said in his heart, "I will not again curse the ground any more for man's sake because the imagination of man's heart is evil from his youth. I will never again strike every living thing, as I have done. [22]While the earth remains, seed time and harvest, and cold and heat, and summer and winter, and day and night will not cease."

Questions & Discoveries

Never Forgotten

What is meant by "God remembered Noah..." (Genesis 8:1)?

Oftentimes, when we (like Noah) execute an order or direction given by God (for instance, when impressed in our spirit by something read or said and supported by an inner spiritual unction confirming it being from God), we do so with a little fear of failure but are confident in God's word and peace. Once we initiate the move and are in the midst of the venture with a committed heart of total reliance on God, we sometimes begin to question, "Where is God?" Though nowhere in Genesis 8 does it imply that was the case with Noah, it also doesn't imply that it wasn't the case with Noah. As a human being, when we make a move of faith based on the word(s) of God, we'd like some sort of sign that He's still with us and that we're on the right track.

Imagine being in the ark, water coming down from the heavens and sky above, as well as springing up from the deep beneath. I'm quite sure that any Navy Sailor can vividly describe to any of us the emotional roller coaster of being on a frigate or destroyer ship in the middle of the ocean when the waves are roaring vehemently. It is far from being smooth sailing, but they must trust the navigation experience of the ship's Captain and the supporting cast of Sailors doing what they're trained to do in such dreadful circumstances.

Now, if Sailors can put their trust in the Captain of the ship (someone who really doesn't know much about any of them personally) to weather a storm and the violent seas in order to accomplish whatever mission, how much more should we trust and believe the God who does know everything about us, and is able not only to help us in weathering the storm and violent seas, but He can speak His peace to calm both? This is the type of faith God saw in Noah when He called Him forth for this mission. Though Noah may have experienced some emotional turbulence during the ride, his faith and trust in God never wavered.

It was Noah's faith and trust in God which caused God to remember him. The Hebrew word for "remember", as used here in Genesis 8:1, is "zâkar" and it means to bring someone to mind and then act on that person's behalf. Acting on Noah's behalf is exactly what God had done, when in the same verse, He caused a wind to pass over the earth for the waters to subside. At the same time, in verse two, He stopped the waters from coming down and the waters from springing up. In 2 Peter 3:9, we learn that God is not slack concerning His promise, as proven in Noah's case. That season of Noah's walk with God was completely based on him exercising the fruits of the spirit – faith, patience, and self-control (Galatians 5:22-23 & Hebrews 11:7). This serves as a reminder and encouragement for us today, knowing that just because at times it may seem we're alone in a project or lifestyle God has called us to, He remembers us and is working behind the scenes for our safe landing and open-door reintroduction. He has a record for remembering and answering those who call upon Him (Genesis 19:29, 30:22, Exodus 6:5, and Psalm 136:23, just to name a few).

The Roaming Raven

Why did Noah send out a raven (Genesis 8:7)?

Although the first mention of clean and unclean animals appears in Genesis 7:2 & 8 when Noah is preparing to enter the ark, Leviticus 11:13-19 distinguished which animals were considered clean and which were considered to be unclean, with ravens being listed as unclean birds. That being the case, it is duly noted that ravens were numbered among the unclean animals depicted in Genesis 7:2 & 8.

The general purpose of unclean animals is for them to clean up the earth or act as scavengers, consuming dead organisms such as animals and plants, which help prevent the spread of diseases. Their primary mission is to seek and devour. Coincidentally, this is the same mission of Satan as spoken of in Job 1:7-8 and 1 Peter 5:8.

Knowing that ravens are scavengers, it beckons the question as to why Noah would send out a raven? Noah sending the raven out first (before the dove) provides a strong indication that he may have been growing impatient from being couped up in an ark with his family and smelly animals, and not hearing any further instruction from God during the outpouring floodwaters and settling of the ark on the mounts of Ararat. Therefore, he acted irrationally and without giving careful thought. Notice how he instantly sent the raven out without a mission, and the raven continued to come and go until the waters were dried from the earth (Genesis 8:7), without serving any purpose that benefited Noah. It wasn't until he came to himself and sensibly sent the dove out with a mission that he started receiving hopeful results. Much like Noah, we too prolong God's answer and direction when we grow impatient and jump ahead of God. It's during such times that God not only uses the silent period to mature the various fruit of the Spirit within us, but also to humble us.

God at Work

What was the significance of God not speaking to Noah until it was time for him and his family to depart the ark (Genesis 8:15)?

Going back to Genesis 8:7-13, we read that Noah irrationally used a raven once and rationally used a dove on three occasions. Afterward, he removed the covering of the ark, looked, and saw the ground was dry. However, it wasn't the results of the dove nor when Noah saw the ground was dry that he was able to depart the ark. It was a month and twenty something days later when the earth was dry (Genesis 8:14), and God began to speak to Noah for he, his family, and the animals to depart the ark (Genesis 8:15-20). Why the wait from the time Noah saw the dry ground until the time God saw the dry earth and directed them to depart? God saw the entire earth as being ready not only for Noah but all the animals (who were to reproduce) as well. Noah was only able to see what would benefit him and his family – God's plans are always much bigger than us.

In answering the lead question, think back to Genesis 8:1 when God remembered Noah and caused the wind to pass over the earth, etc. God doesn't talk just to be talking; He speaks when conditions are right. Because of Him remembering Noah, He was in the process of making the conditions right Himself so that He could speak to Noah with the good news of "Go out of the ship..." In 1 Kings 19:12 we are shown that God isn't revealed in hoopla and anxious responses, but in calmness and peace. As always, He's heavily involved in working behind the scenes, setting the stage for us to be presented. Even in His silence, we're able to learn much because it's during those times that He's doing a work within us or for us.

That Wonderful Smell

Why would burnt offerings please and motivate God to establish a covenant with Himself?

In 1 Samuel 15:22, one of the most profound revelations is provided for us. It says, "Samuel said, "Has the LORD as great delight in burnt offerings and sacrifices, as in obeying the LORD's voice? Behold, to obey is better than sacrifice, and to listen than the fat of rams." This profound information serves as the basis for answering the lead question. God's established covenant to Himself was not because of the burnt offerings presented to Him but the great love He has for mankind. By Noah remembering and reverencing Him through providing burnt offerings, God was able to accept and respect their right relationship as He was mindful of what was to come 2000 years later with the temporal offerings being replaced by the only righteous offering in Jesus. The covenant was made with Himself because He could swear by no one greater (Hebrews 6:13) and He foreknew the ultimate sacrifice of love He would have to give for mankind's complete redemption and reconciliation.

GENESIS 9

Overview

Upon Noah, his family, and all animals and fowl exiting the ark in Genesis 8, this chapter delves into God's pronounced blessings upon Noah and his sons, which not only reflected the instructions God had previously given to Adam and Eve concerning having dominion, but also added: the innate fear of mankind within the animals, fowl, and fish (verse 2); all animals, fowl, and fish being food for mankind (verse 3); and, the required appeasement of life for life among mankind. After pronouncing the blessing, He then established the Noahic covenant between Himself, Noah and his sons, all animals, and fowl which consisted of no massive death for all flesh by water (verse 11); no more flood to destroy the entire earth (verse 11); and the rainbow being established as a sign of the covenant (verses 12-17). Verses 18-29 provide identification of Noah's sons and grandson, the circumstances surrounding a pronounced curse on one of Noah's sons and grandson, and God's blessings upon Noah's other two sons. For this chapter, the following discoveries will be discussed and examined:

1. Why did God allow the innate fear of mankind to exist within the animals, fowl, and fish?

2. Why were Noah, his family and those coming after permitted to eat any animal, fowl, and fish?
3. What is the significance of God using the rainbow as a covenant sign between Him, mankind, all living flesh, and the earth?
4. For what reason did Noah pronounce a curse upon Canaan instead of Ham?

Scriptural Reading

[1]God blessed Noah and his sons, and said to them, "Be fruitful, multiply, and replenish the earth. [2]The fear of you and the dread of you will be on every animal of the earth, and on every bird of the sky. Everything that moves along the ground, and all the fish of the sea, are delivered into your hand. [3]Every moving thing that lives will be food for you. As I gave you the green herb, I have given everything to you. [4]But flesh with its life, that is, its blood, you shall not eat. [5]I will surely require accounting for your life's blood. At the hand of every animal I will require it. At the hand of man, even at the hand of every man's brother, I will require the life of man. [6]Whoever sheds man's blood, his blood will be shed by man, for God made man in his own image. [7]Be fruitful and multiply. Increase abundantly in the earth, and multiply in it."

[8]God spoke to Noah and to his sons with him, saying, [9]"As for me, behold, I establish my covenant with you, and with your offspring after you, [10]and with every living creature that is with you: the birds, the livestock, and every animal of the earth with you, of all that go out of the ship, even every animal of the earth. [11]I will establish my covenant with you: All flesh will not be cut off any more by the waters of the flood. There will never again be a flood to destroy the earth." [12]God said, "This is the token of the covenant which I make between me and you and every living creature that is with you, for perpetual generations: [13]I set my rainbow in the cloud, and it will be a sign of a covenant between me and the earth. [14]When I bring a cloud over the earth, that the rainbow will be seen in the cloud, [15]I will

remember my covenant, which is between me and you and every living creature of all flesh, and the waters will no more become a flood to destroy all flesh. [16]The rainbow will be in the cloud. I will look at it, that I may remember the everlasting covenant between God and every living creature of all flesh that is on the earth." [17]God said to Noah, "This is the token of the covenant which I have established between me and all flesh that is on the earth."

[18]The sons of Noah who went out from the ship were Shem, Ham, and Japheth. Ham is the father of Canaan. [19]These three were the sons of Noah, and from these the whole earth was populated.

[20]Noah began to be a farmer and planted a vineyard. [21]He drank of the wine and got drunk. He was uncovered within his tent. [22]Ham, the father of Canaan, saw the nakedness of his father, and told his two brothers outside. [23]Shem and Japheth took a garment, and laid it on both their shoulders, went in backwards, and covered the nakedness of their father. Their faces were backwards, and they didn't see their father's nakedness. [24]Noah awoke from his wine and knew what his youngest son had done to him.

[25]He said, "Canaan is cursed. He will be a servant of servants to his brothers."

[26]He said, "Blessed be the LORD, the God of Shem. Let Canaan be his servant

[27]May God enlarge Japheth. Let him dwell in the tents of Shem. Let Canaan be his servant."

[28]Noah lived three hundred fifty years after the flood. [29]All the days of Noah were nine hundred fifty years, and then he died.

Questions & Discoveries

Run

Why did God allow the innate fear of mankind to exist within the animals, fowl, and fish (Genesis 9:2)?

In Genesis 9:1-2, we find, upon exiting the ark, Noah and his sons being blessed by God to be fruitful, multiply, and replenish the earth as well as continuing to maintain dominion over all animals, birds, and fish. Unlike God's instructions to Adam in Genesis 1:28 to only have dominion over all animals, birds, and fish, He informs Noah and his sons about the animals, birds, and fish being fearful and dreading them. This isn't something God imposed upon their character; rather, it is a result of the sin of mankind opening the door to affect any and every living flesh made from the ground.

Think back to Genesis 3:10 where it shows how the relationship between man and God was hampered by Adam and Eve fearing God, whereas in times past, they welcomed and reverenced God. Just as the sin nature of mankind promotes a fear of God, so it is the same for those animals, birds, and fish whom mankind was given dominion over. The presumptions of harm, hate, and being found unacceptable are the riddled effects of sin. As stated before, the ramifications of sin spread further than any of us could ever imagine. Why did God allow the innate fear of mankind to exist within the animals, fowl, and fish? It's the eye-opening consequences of a sinful world that created disorder among all facets of God's creation, which can and will only be tamed and brought back on track with the creation of the new heaven and earth as depicted in Revelation 21 and Isaiah 11:6-9.

Free to Eat

Why were Noah, his family, and those coming after permitted to eat any animal, fowl, and fish (Genesis 9:3)?

What makes this such an interesting question is because of what many have learned, believed, and practiced according to what was written within the mosaic law regarding clean and unclean animals. The fact of the matter is that in the beginning, during the days of Adam and Eve being in right standing with God in the garden of Eden, mankind was provided specific dietary instructions as stated in Genesis 1:29, "God said, 'Behold, I have given you every herb yielding seed, which is on the surface of all the earth, and every tree, which bears fruit yielding seed. It will be your food.'" Now, here in Genesis 9:3, it is made very clear that mankind had transitioned from a vegan to an omnivore status either when or sometime after Adam and Eve sinned. In either case, it was permitted by God with the only stipulation being not to eat any meat with the blood in it (Genesis 9:4).

So, why was the change from vegan to omnivore permitted? Mainly due to sin's breakdown of order, which awakened the hungry flesh of man having an appetite for animals as well as the awakened hungry flesh of animals having an appetite for one another – both cases representing unbeatable hunger pangs brought on by the lust of the flesh. Is this to say that God condones sin? Certainly not. The message being relayed is God having mercy on us in our misguided sin-driven free will state. It is also written in 1 Timothy 4:3-5 about us receiving all food with thanksgiving, knowing it is sanctified through the word of God and prayer – which is why grace is said before partaking of a meal. The grace He gives us and the love He shows us is opportunity for us connecting with Him in relationship. The laws we recognize and attempt to abide by are also our stumbling blocks. Our relationship with God isn't dependent on what we eat or what animals are clean and unclean (Matthew 15:11 & Acts 10:10-16). Our relationship with God is built on the foundation of our acceptance and trust in Jesus, which transfers over into us living changed lives in honor of Him and treating others with the same compassion He has for us.

Something of note to be addressed in another volume at a later time, is the fact that it wasn't until Moses came on the scene that restrictions were put in place by God regarding the partaking and restrictions of clean and unclean animals. In Leviticus 11, we find an outline regarding what man was and was not permitted to eat according to the Mosaic law. However, Matthew 15:11 and Acts 10:10-16 makes null and void what was, not by change of God's heart but by proven revelation of what God seeks from us – relationship.

The Glorious Rainbow

What is the significance of God using the rainbow as a covenant sign between Him, mankind, all living flesh, and the earth (Genesis 9:12-17)?

First and most importantly for everyone to know is that whenever God makes a covenant, it is sealed by something that represents Him. What is meant by being sealed? Much like what has been practiced throughout history, every established official and/or office has a seal that represents their authority. An example would be receiving an official piece of correspondence from an official source and recognizing the validity of it by the imprinted seal of authentication. By that document having an official seal intact, it validates the transcribed words as being true and direct and carries the same weight of authority as though verbally stated in-person from the author's own mouth. This has become a standard way of conducting business among mankind, as derived from God's modus operandi.

Typically, throughout scriptures within the Bible, whenever God makes a covenant between Him and mankind, He Himself would be the seal of approval, simply because there's no true and higher authority to legally bind the contract (Hebrews 6:13). Here in Genesis 9:12-17, we read about God's covenant to mankind, all living flesh, and the earth being sealed with the token of the rainbow. So, why the rainbow and how does it fit into representing God?

Firstly, the rainbow reflects His glory as Ezekiel 1:28 makes evident by declaring, "As the appearance of the rainbow that is in the cloud in the day of rain, so was the appearance of the brightness all around. This was the appearance of the likeness of the LORD's glory. When I saw it, I fell on my face, and I heard a voice of one that spoke." Secondly, the rainbow reflects His position of power as Revelation 4:2-3 illustrates, "Immediately I was in the Spirit. Behold, there was a throne set in heaven, and one sitting on the throne that looked like a jasper stone and a sardius. There was a rainbow around the throne, like an emerald to look at." Lastly, the rainbow reflects His presence as Revelation 10:1 presents, "I saw a mighty angel coming down out of the sky, clothed with a cloud. A rainbow was on his head. His face was like the sun, and his feet like pillars of fire."

All aspects of the rainbow (His glory, His power, and His presence) represent His seal of approval for carrying out the words He bound Himself to in remembering to never cut off all flesh by the waters of the flood. The rainbow in the clouds is something that can't be altered in any way, fashion, or form – we know that Jesus (the living Word of God) is the same yesterday, today, and forever (Hebrews 13:8).

More than Nakedness

For what reason did Noah pronounce a curse upon Canaan instead of Ham (Genesis 9:22-27)?

Upon exiting the ark starting in verse 18, we are reintroduced to Noah's sons Shem, Ham and Japheth. However, in that same verse we learn of Ham being the father of Canaan (who would be Noah's grandson). It's somewhat interesting because no other grandchild is mentioned by Noah's other sons, Shem and Japheth. As we continue reading, there's an incident that occurs where Noah gets a little "tipsy" (i.e. drunk) and Ham happened to stumble upon Noah in his tent, saw his nakedness, and shared what he saw with his two brothers, Shem and Japheth. Unlike Ham, the two brothers walked in backwards and covered their father. When Noah awakes, he was aware of what Ham had done and proceeds to curse Canaan. Very interesting, huh? Ham sinned, but Canaan was cursed.

Let's take a deeper look at what happened, which led to Canaan being cursed. In reading that Ham saw his father's nakedness, most will think Ham saw his father in the nude. That was far from what happened here. In Genesis 9:22, the Hebrew word for "nakedness" is "`erwāh" and it actually means "shameful nakedness" indicating immoral behavior, whereas the Hebrew word for describing simple nakedness or bareness (nudity) is "`eyrōm", which describes naked in terms of Adam and Eve when they ate of the forbidden fruit. Notice that in Genesis 9:18, Canaan is mentioned as being the son of Ham. It is a strong inclination that Canaan was somehow involved in immoral behavior with his drunken grandfather, and Ham was indirectly to blame because he was

Canaan's father and knew of what had taken place. With that being the circumstance and since Noah was the violated victim, he had every right to step in and execute judgement on Ham's son, Canaan. Scripture states that Shem and Japheth did not see their father's nakedness, which signifies they never mentioned nor made mockery of what transpired.

Remember when Adam and Eve sinned, and God issued them just penalties as connected to their actions (Genesis 3)? Noah followed suit by doing the same. Since Ham and/or Canaan saw fit to serve themselves by committing immoral acts with Noah, Canaan's penalty was for him and his offspring to be a servant of servants to the blessed Shem and Japheth and their offspring for many generations to come. This was a penalty that not only Canaan had to bear, but served as a curse of shame for Ham to live with for the rest of his life.

GENESIS 10

Overview

In this chapter, we are presented with what has become known as "Table of Nations", which lists the descendants of Japheth, Shem, and Ham as the patriarchal founders of seventy nations. According to biblestudy.org, "The table of nations categorizes people and lands into three families: Japheth, Shem, and Ham based on racial descent, geographical location, language differences, or political units." While there is much information we can glean from this chapter regarding historical origins, we will continue to look at it through the lens of noticeable ponderings based on what is read in the textual content provided. The following discoveries will be discussed and examined:

1. What does Nimrod represent as a mighty hunter before the LORD?
2. What's the connection between Noah's nakedness incident and Canaan's lineage?
3. What is meant by the earth being divided in the days of Peleg?
4. What are some of the nation's names originating from the lineages of Japheth, Shem, and Ham?

Scriptural Reading

[1]Now this is the history of the generations of the sons of Noah and of Shem, Ham, and Japheth. Sons were born to them after the flood.

[2]The sons of Japheth were: Gomer, Magog, Madai, Javan, Tubal, Meshech, and Tiras. [3]The sons of Gomer were: Ashkenaz, Riphath, and Togarmah. [4]The sons of Javan were: Elishah, Tarshish, Kittim, and Dodanim. [5]Of these were the islands of the nations divided in their lands, everyone after his language, after their families, in their nations.

[6]The sons of Ham were: Cush, Mizraim, Put, and Canaan. [7]The sons of Cush were: Seba, Havilah, Sabtah, Raamah, and Sabteca. The sons of Raamah were: Sheba and Dedan. [8]Cush became the father of Nimrod. He began to be a mighty one in the earth. [9]He was a mighty hunter before the LORD. Therefore it is said, "like Nimrod, a mighty hunter before the LORD". [10]The beginning of his kingdom was Babel, Erech, Accad, and Calneh, in the land of Shinar. [11]Out of that land he went into Assyria, and built Nineveh, Rehoboth Ir, Calah, [12]and Resen between Nineveh and the great city Calah. [13]Mizraim became the father of Ludim, Anamim, Lehabim, Naphtuhim, [14]Pathrusim, Casluhim (which the Philistines descended from), and Caphtorim.

[15]Canaan became the father of Sidon (his firstborn), Heth, [16]the Jebusites, the Amorites, the Girgashites, [17]the Hivites, the Arkites, the Sinites, [18]the Arvadites, the Zemarites, and the Hamathites. Afterward the families of the Canaanites were spread abroad. [19]The border of the Canaanites was from Sidon—as you go toward Gerar—to Gaza—as you go toward Sodom, Gomorrah, Admah, and Zeboiim—to Lasha. [20]These are the sons of Ham, after their families, according to their languages, in their lands and their nations.

[21]Children were also born to Shem (the elder brother of Japheth), the father of all the children of Eber. [22]The sons of Shem were: Elam, Asshur, Arpachshad, Lud, and Aram. [23]The sons of Aram were: Uz, Hul, Gether, and Mash. [24]Arpachshad

became the father of Shelah. Shelah became the father of Eber. [25]To Eber were born two sons. The name of the one was Peleg, for in his days the earth was divided. His brother's name was Joktan. [26]Joktan became the father of Almodad, Sheleph, Hazarmaveth, Jerah, [27]Hadoram, Uzal, Diklah, [28]Obal, Abimael, Sheba, [29]Ophir, Havilah, and Jobab. All these were the sons of Joktan. [30]Their dwelling extended from Mesha, as you go toward Sephar, the mountain of the east. [31]These are the sons of Shem, by their families, according to their languages, lands, and nations.

[32]These are the families of the sons of Noah, by their generations, according to their nations. The nations divided from these in the earth after the flood.

Questions & Discoveries

Hot to Trot

What does Nimrod represent as a mighty hunter before the LORD (Genesis 10:8-12)?

Interestingly as clearly annotated in scriptures, Nimrod is linked to Cush but not readily listed and identified as one of his sons in the same sentences as the rest are. Instead, in both areas of scripture (Genesis 10:7-8 and 1 Chronicles 1:9-10), Nimrod's name appears separately as Cush "becoming" the father of him (or "begetting"), which strongly implies the possibility of Cush simply being a father figure to him rather than his direct biological father. In either case, the impression Cush had upon Nimrod was reflected in how Nimrod lived.

For starters, in Hebrew the name "Cush" means "hot", with the connotation of being one who operates emotionally and suddenly – sort of unhinged. Notice what is mentioned at the end of verse 8 concerning Nimrod: "he began to be a mighty one in the earth." This may be the result of the impact Cush had upon him as being hot-headed. He (Nimrod) had honed and developed himself into a "mighty hunter" (Genesis 10:9). His being a "mighty hunter" wasn't just a compliment to his skillset, but an indication of his becoming a violent bully without regard for God. Being called a "mighty hunter before the LORD" revealed that he considered himself as a god and in competition with God. This is confirmed in verse 10, which sets forth him establishing his "kingdom", as well as the building of the tower of Babel as mentioned in Genesis 11:1-9.

Lastly, the term "nimrod" can be positively and negatively defined. According to Merriam-Webster online dictionary, nimrod is defined as being either "a skillful hunter" or "a foolish or inept person", and Nimrod identified with both. He possessed an unmatched talent governed by an unbridled quick temper. On another note, if by chance Cush was not his biological father, the study of Nimrod proves how important it is for biological fathers to be actively involved in their children's lives. See, Cush could only instill in Nimrod that which was seen by his actions, but a biological father possesses the authority of corrective action that is needed in the lives of young men. Without a harness of authority, young men are prone to become might hunters before the LORD.

Connecting the Dots

What's the connection between Noah's nakedness incident and Canaan's lineage (Genesis 9:22-24 & 10:19)?

During our final review of Genesis 9:22-24, there was the story of Ham "seeing" Noah's "nakedness", but Canaan receiving the curse as pronounced by Noah. We delved into understanding the translation of "nakedness" as meaning "immoral behavior", which in some form or another was an act of violation against Noah by either Ham and/or Canaan (with the effects signifying Canaan as being the actual perpetrator). As we pick it up here in Genesis 10, we first learn that Ham had four sons (Cush, Mizraim, Put, and Canaan) mentioned in verse 6; however, Canaan received the curse and not any of the other sons. This provides further proof that Canaan was somehow involved with Noah's nakedness incident.

The remaining evidence of Canaan's involvement and the curse being justly pronounced upon him is revealed in Genesis 10:19.

It's in this particular verse where we find the immoral behavior and sin nature of Canaan as manifested in the borders of the Canaanites, namely the cities of Sodom and Gomorrah. Sodom and Gomorrah had become two of the most wicked, immoral places ever, and notoriously known throughout all scriptures. The Hebrew meaning of "Sodom" is "burnt or scorching"; and the Hebrew meaning of "Gomorrah" is "submersion". Both cities represented the possessing of unquenchable and unrestrained wicked desires and lascivious lifestyles as depicted in Genesis 18 and 19. They were the epitome of liberated immoral behavior – stemming from the sin nature of Canaan.

Later in scripture we find that not only did Noah have to deal with Canaan serving his desires by cursing him to be the lowliest of servants, but God eventually had to deal with the deep-rooted sinful and immoral behavior by completely obliterating Sodom and Gomorrah (Genesis 19:23-29) and pronouncing a curse upon the land where they once were (Deuteronomy 29:23). As we've been learning and seeing repeatedly throughout this publication, a little sin has far-reaching ramifications.

Unhinged

What is meant by the earth being divided in the days of Peleg (Genesis 10:25)?

To answer this lead question, we must jump ahead to Genesis 11. In the beginning of that chapter, we read about the people being of one language, the tower of Babel being built, God destroying it, and creating various languages among them, causing the people to be dispersed throughout the earth. Reading down a little further to Genesis 11:16, it's where we find the birth of Peleg and can understand the reason behind the Hebrew meaning of his name, which is "divided." He was born during the time that divided languages were instituted by God. More information surrounding the circumstances will be discussed in the study of Genesis 11. The answer to, "What is meant by the earth being divided in the days of

Peleg?" is in reference to languages and the dispersing of people throughout the earth.

The Birth of Nations

What are some of the nation's names originating from the lineages of Japheth, Shem, and Ham (Genesis 10)?

Guess what? I have some difficult news to share, and that is that Ancestry.com and other genealogical agents are not the first to provide discoveries of ancestor matches. Biblically, ancestral lineages have long been documented since the beginning of time as we know it. For your entertainment, here are a few traces of origins that are found within this chapter of Genesis splintering from Japheth, Shem, and Ham, and based on the names of some of their sons:

Shem: Israel, Syria, Lebanon, Assyria, Iraq, Iran, Pakistan, and Afghanistan
Ham: Algeria, Libya, Egypt, Sudan, Yemen, Saudi Arabia, and Israel/Palestine
Japheth: Ukraine, Russia, Greece, Turkey, Armenia, Cyprus, and Georgia

GENESIS 11

Overview

This chapter presents the post-ark trifecta of God's will for mankind consisting of mankind being dispersed throughout the earth, establishing and focusing on the direct lineage from which Jesus would come centuries later, and, most notably, the introduction of Abram (Abraham) who would become the father of faith, affecting Christian believers throughout the world and throughout all generations. We're provided behind the scenes circumstances that led to God instituting various languages as well as a detailed recording of Shem's family record consisting of the foundation of early semitic persons from which the Hebrew nation would be birthed. The following discoveries will be discussed and examined:

1. Why did God consider being one people and having one language an offense (Genesis 11:6-7)?
2. Why was the focus solely on Shem's lineage, excluding Japheth and Ham (Genesis 11:10-27)?
3. Were Abram, Nahor, and Haran born as triplets (Genesis 11:26)?
4. What is the significance of Terah dying in Haran (Genesis 11:32)?

Scriptural Reading

[1]The whole earth was of one language and of one speech. [2]As they traveled east, they found a plain in the land of Shinar, and they lived there. [3]They said to one another, "Come, let's make bricks, and burn them thoroughly." They had brick for stone, and they used tar for mortar. [4]They said, "Come, let's build ourselves a city, and a tower whose top reaches to the sky, and let's make a name for ourselves, lest we be scattered abroad on the surface of the whole earth."

[5]The LORD came down to see the city and the tower, which the children of men built. [6]The LORD said, "Behold, they are one people, and they all have one language, and this is what they begin to do. Now nothing will be withheld from them, which they intend to do. [7]Come, let's go down, and there confuse their language, that they may not understand one another's speech."

[8]So the LORD scattered them abroad from there on the surface of all the earth. They stopped building the city. [9]Therefore its name was called Babel, because there the LORD confused the language of all the earth. From there, the LORD scattered them abroad on the surface of all the earth.

[10]This is the history of the generations of Shem: Shem was one hundred years old when he became the father of Arpachshad two years after the flood. [11]Shem lived five hundred years after he became the father of Arpachshad and became the father of more sons and daughters.

[12]Arpachshad lived thirty-five years and became the father of Shelah. [13]Arpachshad lived four hundred three years after he became the father of Shelah and became the father of more sons and daughters.

[14]Shelah lived thirty years and became the father of Eber. [15]Shelah lived four hundred three years after he became the father of Eber and became the father of more sons and daughters.

[16]Eber lived thirty-four years and became the father of Peleg. [17]Eber lived four hundred thirty years after he became the father of Peleg and became the father of more sons and daughters.

¹⁸Peleg lived thirty years and became the father of Reu. ¹⁹Peleg lived two hundred nine years after he became the father of Reu and became the father of more sons and daughters.

²⁰Reu lived thirty-two years and became the father of Serug. ²¹Reu lived two hundred seven years after he became the father of Serug and became the father of more sons and daughters.

²²Serug lived thirty years and became the father of Nahor. ²³Serug lived two hundred years after he became the father of Nahor and became the father of more sons and daughters.

²⁴Nahor lived twenty-nine years and became the father of Terah. ²⁵Nahor lived one hundred nineteen years after he became the father of Terah and became the father of more sons and daughters.

²⁶Terah lived seventy years, and became the father of Abram, Nahor, and Haran.

²⁷Now this is the history of the generations of Terah. Terah became the father of Abram, Nahor, and Haran. Haran became the father of Lot. ²⁸Haran died in the land of his birth, in Ur of the Chaldees, while his father Terah was still alive. ²⁹Abram and Nahor married wives. The name of Abram's wife was Sarai, and the name of Nahor's wife was Milcah, the daughter of Haran, who was also the father of Iscah. ³⁰Sarai was barren. She had no child. ³¹Terah took Abram his son, Lot the son of Haran, his son's son, and Sarai his daughter-in-law, his son Abram's wife. They went from Ur of the Chaldees, to go into the land of Canaan. They came to Haran and lived there. ³²The days of Terah were two hundred five years. Terah died in Haran.

Questions & Discoveries

The Beauty of Diversity

Why did God consider being one people and having one language an offense (Genesis 11:6-7)?

In Genesis 11:1-5, we're painted a poignant picture of what mankind had become in a few generations from when Noah and his family departed the ark. It's a picture that does not include anything about anyone following and/or walking with God; it's about a people who had come together collectively in imagination, work, pride and rebellion. This is after God had made an irreversible covenant with Noah and his sons, the earth, and all living flesh to never destroy the earth with floodwaters again (Genesis 9:8-17). And it's also after His commandment for mankind to "Be fruitful and multiply. Increase abundantly in the earth, and multiply in it." (Genesis 9:7).

So often mankind wants to remind and hold God accountable to His covenant and promises with fervent expectancy but are quick to flagrantly dismiss His commandment(s). Genesis 11:6-7 proves to be no different. With them possibly remembering His covenant to not kill them, they capitalized upon it as an opportunity to defy Him. They refused to be fruitful (become diverse) and multiply. They refused to increase abundantly in the earth, and multiply in it. They chose to connect with God on their terms and that was by them making a name for themselves, attempting to be on the same level as God, and uniting to be comfortably stationary in rebellion rather than dispersing to fulfill God's plan.

Some may ask, "What's the harm in that?" Firstly, they defied God's commandment. Secondly, they took for granted God's covenant. Thirdly, they were following the comfortable, deceptive plan of the enemy in pleasing the flesh. Ignorantly led by their selfish sin nature, brought on by Satan, they were attempting to abort their lives by foregoing God's purpose and plan. God's plan was for the entire earth to be filled and blessed with His creation (mankind) in various forms of peoples, nations, languages, etc. Why? Because the intent was for God's glory to be represented by the reproductive offspring of mankind by way of the seeds He placed in mankind.

Having one people and one language only limited the talents and giftings God had placed in each of them. Those talents and gifts could never grow into fruition when planted in the same soil as everyone else. Different talents and gifts planted and nurtured in various areas, conducive to their growth, produces the immeasurable beauty of who and what God represents, accordingly. That was an offense to God just as most parents would be offended by their children, whom they properly raised and paid the cost for them attending college in preparation for a career, if instead their children chose to stay at home (jobless) after being equipped for life. God doesn't want to control any of us, He simply wants what's planted within us to be manifested, useful, and appreciated for Him and others to benefit from with joy.

All About Who Was to Come

Why was the focus solely on Shem's lineage, excluding Japheth and Ham (Genesis 11:10-27)?

The most simplistic and truthful answer to the lead question is that it was through Shem's lineage that Jesus came, in Whom we have redemption and reconciliation with God. The surety of Shem's lineage, being a direct link to and through Abraham and David to Jesus, was Mary's lineage being traced back to David through his son, Nathan (Luke 3), and Joseph's lineage being traced back to David through his son, Solomon (Matthew 1) – both lineages being generations apart from one another, but all leading back to Shem. This covered all prophecies of Jesus' coming through the line of David according to Jeremiah 23:5-6, Isaiah 7:14, Isaiah 9:7 and many others.

In no way does this insinuate that the lineages of Japheth and Ham are irrelevant. The design and intent of God giving us His written word is to map us in the direction of Jesus for salvation. Jesus came for the benefit of all mankind (John 3:16), including the descendants of Japheth and Ham.

The irony in Jesus coming through Shem's lineage is the fact that the Hebrew translation of "Shem" is "name", and the Greek translation of "Jesus" is "Jehovah is salvation". In Acts 4:12, Peter declares (concerning Jesus), "There is salvation in no one else, for there is no other name under heaven that is given among men, by which we must be saved!" In other words, while Shem was able to introduce and institute a temporal pattern for carrying out a relationship with God, his name, like the many patriarchs before and after him, could in no way measure up to the only worthy name of Jesus. Jesus's name takes us out of the business of working for a relationship with God, and places us into a right relationship with God.

Who's Who?

Were Abram, Nahor, and Haran born as triplets (Genesis 11:26)?

In Genesis 11:26, we read that at the age of 70, Terah had three sons: Abram, Nahor, and Haran. Oftentimes, this verse is taken to mean that they were born as triplets, and that Abram was the elder. Guess what? Both perceptions are incorrect. Most times (such as the case here) in scripture, when the lineage of Jesus is mentioned, the person in His direct lineage is respectfully mentioned first (as accustomed by the writers), which is why Abram is mentioned first. Now, let's take a look at Genesis 11:32 and Genesis 12:4. In Genesis 11:32, we see that Terah died at the age of 205 years. In Genesis 12:4, we see that Abram is 75 years old when he departs from Haran (following Terah's death). Doing a little thing called subtraction (205 (Terah's age at death) minus 75 (Abram's age at Terah's death), we're left with the number 130, which represents the age of Terah during Abram's birth.

Genesis 11:26 can and is easily misunderstood by many. Although it reads, "Terah lived seventy years, and became the father of Abram, Nahor, and Haran", the implication is that at age 70 three sons were born to him, with Haran being the firstborn followed by Nahor and the youngest being Abram. In Genesis 11:28, we learn that Haran (the eldest brother) dies. With Nahor being older than Abram, it was incumbent upon Abram (the youngest son) to reside with Terah (their father) along with Lot (Haran's son) out of customary obligation as Terah's responsibility. This also explains why Terah took Abram, Sarai, and Lot with him to the land of Haran and did not take Nahor (the eldest son) and his wife. This proves the actual chronological order of birth as Haran (1st born), Nahor (2nd born), and Abram (the youngest).

Trapped

What is the significance of Terah dying in Haran (Genesis 11:32)?

Ironically, after Haran dies in the land of Ur of the Chaldees (Genesis 11:28), Terah gathers the family to move from there and into a city called Haran, where he (Terah) dies (Genesis 11:32). As most parents can relate, although the loss of any child introduces saddened and mixed emotions, there is something very formidable and unexplainable about the emotions experienced during the loss of a firstborn and youngest born. Their demise can be unshakeable, mainly because it is something unimaginable experience for a parent – something that catches you not only off guard by what happened, but off guard by the timing of it happening. Most of us view a full life as being when the children are alive to bury the parents versus the parents witnessing their children passing first.

Rightfully so, Terah loved his son, Haran, and even took guardianship over Lot (Haran's son) after his death. More than likely, Lot modeled Haran either by appearance or mannerisms, in a way that reminded Terah of Haran, but he could never replace Haran. The implication of Terah moving from the place where Haran died (Ur of the Chaldees) to a place named "Haran" and dying there, is that the pain and depression were overwhelming and devastatingly affected him from the time Haran died until the time of his own death.

Although speculative, many may view the older sibling as typically being more adventurous, with a hunger for experiencing various appetites of life – they're the risk takers, who oftentimes may have good intentions but choose to hang with the wrong crowd. This may have served as the detrimental reason behind Haran's death. Also, it may indicate why Lot followed along the same path he had chosen in Genesis 13:10-11, and needed to be saved from the destruction coming upon Sodom and Gomorrah (Genesis 19), thanks to the intervention of Abraham (Genesis 18).

SECTION II

Revelation 1 - 11

REVELATION 1

Overview

The book of Revelation is one that is rarely discussed and/or taught in the church. Certain scriptures may be quoted here and there, but it's not a book many church leaders (i.e., apostles, prophets, evangelists, pastors, and teachers) either feel comfortable teaching or are equipped to teach. That is not a knock, rather it is pure fact about most churches. Nonetheless, as we trek through chapters one through 11, there will be questions and discoveries addressed regarding certain scriptures many may have read, heard, or pondered.

Let's begin with understanding the transliteration of the word "revelation" which derives from its Greek origin "apokálypsis" and means to "unveil" or "uncover". What is being uncovered for us in this book is the proper context regarding a myriad of spiritual and natural matters as they relate to what was, what is, and what is to come. In this chapter, we're introduced to the author, purpose, and divine execution of prophetic messages. Additionally, this chapter sets the stage by unveiling and connecting the foundational pieces from which the remaining 21 chapters will be built. In this chapter, the following questions and discoveries will be examined:

1. What is the significance of the revelation being given to Jesus by God?
2. Who are those represented in the salutation John delivers?
3. How do we exemplify being a kingdom of priests to God?
4. How will everyone be able to see Jesus coming with the clouds?
5. What is meant by being "in the Spirit"?
6. Are these scriptures describing Jesus literally or metaphorically?
7. What are the significances of the seven angels and the seven churches?

Scriptural Reading

¹This is the Revelation of Jesus Christ, which God gave Him to show to his servants the things which must happen soon, which he sent and made known by his angel to his servant, John, ²who testified to God's word and of the testimony of Jesus Christ, about everything that he saw.
³Blessed is he who reads and those who hear the words of the prophecy, and keep the things that are written in it, for the time is near.
⁴John, to the seven assemblies that are in Asia: Grace to you and peace from God, who is and who was and who is to come; and from the seven Spirits who are before his throne; ⁵and from Jesus Christ, the faithful witness, the firstborn of the dead, and the ruler of the kings of the earth. To him who loves us and washed us from our sins by his blood— ⁶and he made us to be a Kingdom, priests to his God and Father—to him be the glory and the dominion forever and ever. Amen.
⁷Behold, he is coming with the clouds, and every eye will see him, including those who pierced him. All the tribes of the earth will mourn over him. Even so, Amen.
⁸"I am the Alpha and the Omega," says the Lord God, "who is and who was and who is to come, the Almighty."
⁹I John, your brother and partner with you in the oppression, Kingdom, and perseverance in Christ Jesus, was on the isle that

is called Patmos because of God's Word and the testimony of Jesus Christ. [10]I was in the Spirit on the Lord's Day, and I heard behind me a loud voice, like a trumpet [11]saying, "What you see, write in a book and send to the seven assemblies: to Ephesus, Smyrna, Pergamum, Thyatira, Sardis, Philadelphia, and to Laodicea."

[12]I turned to see the voice that spoke with me. Having turned, I saw seven golden lamp stands. [13]And among the lamp stands was one like a son of man, clothed with a robe reaching down to his feet, and with a golden sash around his chest. [14]His head and his hair were white as white wool, like snow. His eyes were like a flame of fire. [15]His feet were like burnished brass, as if it had been refined in a furnace. His voice was like the voice of many waters. [16]He had seven stars in his right hand. Out of his mouth proceeded a sharp two-edged sword. His face was like the sun shining at its brightest. [17]When I saw him, I fell at his feet like a dead man. He laid his right hand on me, saying, "Don't be afraid. I am the first and the last, [18]and the Living one. I was dead, and behold, I am alive forever and ever. Amen. I have the keys of Death and of Hades. [19]Write therefore the things which you have seen, and the things which are, and the things which will happen hereafter. [20]The mystery of the seven stars which you saw in my right hand, and the seven golden lamp stands is this: The seven stars are the angels of the seven assemblies. The seven lamp stands are seven assemblies.

Questions & Discovery

Making it Plain

What is the significance of the revelation being given to Jesus by God (Revelation 1:1)?

The opening introduction of Revelation 1:1 clearly identifies this book as being the unveiling or uncovering of Jesus Christ, signifying the entirety of events exemplifying His purpose – not only as Him (Jesus) being the living word of God, but also as the savior for all mankind.   The significance of God "giving" Jesus the revelation of who He (Jesus) is, is not an indication that Jesus did not know who He was and is, rather it is God disclosing the anointed purpose of Jesus as He "bestowed" upon Him as His sinless spoken word – being the second Adam for spiritual salvation (1 Corinthians 15:45 & 47). In other words, the first portion of Revelation 1:1 should be read as, "This is the uncovering of Jesus' anointed purpose, which God bestowed upon Him…"

The Triune Salutation

Who are those represented in the salutation John delivers (Revelation 1:4-6)?

In verses four through six, John starts with a salutation to an audience of believers (those represented within the seven churches) as he begins to relay the divine revelatory prophecy, which he received and had been instructed to share.   It's within that salutation that interesting information is found. Firstly, he starts with the granting of grace and peace to the audience from "God, who is, and who was, and who is to come." The Greek transliteration for the word "grace" (as mentioned in verse 4) is "cháris", and it means "unearned or unmerited favor". It signifies God bestowing favor or blessing as a gift to the audience of believers without expectation of return nor any required work on their part. Most importantly, it's a greeting from God to repentant sinners who not only received their sins being forgiven, but they also have a relationship with Him. By them (us) having a relationship with Him, He greets them (us) with the blessing of presenting the knowledge (revelation) of what was, is, and is to come – sharing detailed events for the ears of family only.

This brings us to three points of how God is recognized within this salutation in relation to the various relationships the audience has with Him. For some, He is seen as the God who is – representing a "now" or "present-day" relationship with Him. For some, He is seen as the God who was – representing a "used to" or a "doubtful" relationship with Him. Still for some, He is seen as the God who is to come – representing a "hopeful" relationship with Him. As many of us have learned from Exodus 3:14, He is "I AM THAT I AM," which in the Hebrew transliteration means "I am He who exists" – regardless of how we view and/or experience a relationship with Him, it doesn't change His everlasting presence, nor His grace and peace extended toward us. .

Secondly, we read the same grace and peace being given to us from the "seven Spirits which are before his throne." Biblically, most times when the number seven is referenced in scriptures, it metaphorically carries the connotation of "perfection", and here in the latter part of verse four, it remains the same. Seven or "perfection" implies nothing missing and/or blemishing, and such is the Spirit of God. It's an entity which holds the full equal authority, will, and power of God as represented here throughout the seven churches (aka, the overall big Church which all believers are a part of in Jesus). It's that same Spirit that the Apostle Paul mentions which confirms our identity in Romans 8:16, "The Spirit himself testifies with our spirit that we are children of God." It's how we receive confirmation of God's grace and peace.

Lastly, in verse 5, we find the same grace and peace being given to us from Jesus the Christ, whose résumé includes being the faithful witness, the firstborn of the dead, and the ruler of the kings of the earth. In other words, for us believers who have repented of our sinfulness and accepted His forgiveness, Jesus is extending delight and joy in us knowing that His faithfulness wasn't in vain, knowing that He was the firstborn of the dead who opened the door for a host of millions (possibly billions) to rise and join Him, and, knowing that He is the righteous ruler of the kings of the earth that is and that is to come.

NOTE: pertaining to the seven churches and seven Spirits, more will be addressed as we proceed throughout the remaining 10 chapters.

Peculiar Servants

How do we exemplify being a kingdom of priests to God (Revelation 1:6)?

Exodus 19:5-6 and 1 Peter 2:9 offer the best answers for this lead question. It reads:

"Now therefore, if you will indeed obey my voice and keep my covenant, then you shall be my own possession from among all peoples; for all the earth is mine; and you shall be to me a kingdom of priests and a holy nation." -Exodus 19:5-6

"But you are a chosen race, a royal priesthood, a holy nation, a people for God's own possession, that you may proclaim the excellence of Him who called you out of darkness into his marvelous light." -1 Peter 2:9

What makes believers a kingdom of priests to God is not measured by the amount of material wealth and/or possessions. It's having a humbled heart to realize the need for His love, mercy, grace, and salvation from our sinful natures. It's utilizing the measure of faith given each of us to accept the reconciliation of peace He has provided through the sacrifice of Jesus. In doing so, our lives metamorphosize from being recognized as practicing and doomed sinners to being spirit-filled followers of Jesus (Christians). When that occurs, we then become a kingdom of priests with characteristics of being humble, obedient, and covenant keepers. Humble, as to not think more highly of ourselves than we ought to (Romans 12:3) by seeing Him as the one and only true God. Obedient, by trusting Him (Proverbs 3:5) to lead and guide us. Covenant keepers, by being mindful of His covenant with us (Hebrews 8:10-13), realizing it's not dependent on our works, but His word. These are what signify His children as being a kingdom of priests to Himself – our lifestyles reflect godliness rather than worldlines.

God's Glory

How will everyone be able to see Jesus coming with the clouds (Revelation 1:7)?

In Revelation 1:7, we (as believers) are presented with the telling sign welcoming of Jesus' return. For many this will be a gloriously joy-filled moment, but for others it will be a not-so-happy day. This verse provides a declarative prelude illustrating how He will appear (with clouds) and to whom He will appear (to everyone). There will be those who will mourn (joyfully) over the sight of His arrival just as there will be those who will mourn (sorrowfully) over the sight of His arrival. Those who will be experiencing a sense of joy during such time are they who trusted and believed in Him. Those who will experience great sorrow are they who doubted His existence, rejected His calling, walked in the ways of this world, and/or saw themselves as their own gods.

While Revelation 1:7 introduces us to Jesus' second coming, Revelation 20:11-15 and 22:12-14 make clear to us the reason for His second coming – to justly execute a distribution of judgements and rewards for all mankind (His followers and non-followers). What do these details have to do with the lead question? Collectively, they bring us to a place and time which affords everyone a front row seat to witness the most glorious and unimaginable scene there ever was or will be – the return of Jesus with the clouds (sitting on a white throne (Revelation 20:11)). We're told that, "…every eye will see Him, including those who pierced Him." How is it possible for every eye to see Him, and what is the significance of "including those who pierced Him"?

Firstly, let's look at a couple of extraordinary transformations that must occur for every eye to see Him. This includes opening the eyes of those who are or have been physically and/or spiritually blinded, as well as those who have physically and spiritually died. It also includes those "who pierced Him", which symbolizes not only those of us who received Him as Lord and Savior, but also those who knew of Him and failed to receive and maintain a relationship with Him. This act of "piercing" is the same as that spoken of in Zechariah 12:10 and John 19:31-37, which was/is performed by both Jews and Gentiles. It represents the fullness of mankind's sin nature, pricking the perfect and sinless sacrifice of Jesus – Him becoming the sin atonement on our behalf (1 John 2:1-2 & 1 Peter 2:24). In return, Jesus, having given His life, continually poured out His spirit of grace and supplication (prayers) for reconciliation on our behalf. Bottom line: those "who pierced Him" are those who know Him as Lord and Savior, and those who perceive Him as the Son of God, but rejected Him as their Lord and Savior.

Those couple of background points needed to be made to provide clarity to how every eye would be able to see Him with the clouds. Unlike how many may perceive this occurring in the natural world with everyone being in their respective geographic regions, this will be a spiritual gathering of souls from all over the world, times past and present, dead and alive, etc. We will all be summoned at a particular place in time to stand before the King of Kings as we all see and witness His glorious arrival as Judge and Lord. Everyone shall behold the beauty of His majesty. Just as it is procedural respect for everyone to be already in place prior to the arrival of prominent leaders of nations, organizations, etc. being received as guests of honor, so it will be for the arrival of the King of Kings. This is the God-set standard protocol (Philippians 2:9-11) for all creation in reverencing His Excellency, He Who is Holy, and Mighty above all. All eyes (billions) will be affixed upon Him without any need for satellite assistance or scientific magnifications.

Submerged

What is meant by being "in the Spirit" (Revelation 1:10)?

There are many of us "seasoned" believers who have heard and/or witnessed someone being "in the Spirit." It was identified as such based on some strange phenomena occurring during a church service, especially within Pentecostal and charismatic denominations. That phenomena may have been or can be uncontrollable laughter, spontaneously running marathon-type laps around the church, "speaking in tongues", etc. Though scripturally unfounded, it was (and still is) promoted as being "proof" of God's presence in these particular places of worship. However, as we mature in the word of God, we come to learn and know that all things guided by God's Spirit are done "decently and in order" (1 Corinthians 14:40), which allows for His Spirit to work through us properly by using His giftings.

The Spirit of God working through us is completely different from someone being "in the Spirit." In the New Testament there are at least six occasions that provide examples of being "in the Spirit": Acts 10:10, 2 Corinthians 12:2, Revelation 1:10, 4:2, 17:3, and 21:10. During each occasion, being "in the Spirit" was not something sought after, rather it was solely God's doing. Each instance was depicted as the person being in a fourth dimensional type trance, which involved them being completely submerged and consumed by the Spirit – God having full control of revealing time, location, and actions. While in such a state, a spiritual "time-travel" took place, bringing them to either a future event and/or providing deeper revelation and understanding of a matter. In Acts 10:10-15, Peter was submerged in a trance (in the Spirit) for the purpose of receiving clarity about Jesus' salvation being extended to all mankind (Jews and Gentiles). In 2 Corinthians 12:1-9, Paul was submerged in a trance (in the Spirit) for the purpose of being made humble and understanding God's grace, as well as being an encouragement to other believers. And in Revelation 1:10, 4:2, 17:3, and 21:10, John was submerged "in the Spirit" (a trance) for the purpose of receiving behind the scenes historical and future revelations for encouraging believers.

The essence of being "in the Spirit" is for God to reveal something for the greater benefit of all believers. It is not something we can jump on board for obtaining, just because. Being "in the Spirit" is a place God initiates and positions a person for according to His will and always for a greater purpose that affects the entire family of believers.

The Descriptive Message

Are these scriptures describing Jesus literally or metaphorically (Revelation 1:14-15)?

Oftentimes people will read the Bible and interpret all scriptures as literal, without giving a second thought of praying for understanding, researching scriptures with appropriate Biblical reference material, or seeking out knowledgeable ministerial support. They'll read what is stated and run with the misinterpreted information as though they're the chosen one God is entrusting with His word for the spreading of misinformation. For starters, know that God is NOT the author of confusion (1 Corinthians 14:33). Sadly, more often than I care to admit, I have heard the misinterpreted information posed in Revelation 1:14-15 as supposed "proof" of Jesus' ethnicity. What these scriptures provide is much deeper than the superficial nonsense concerning race. These scriptures provide a metaphorical revelation of Jesus as being the first and the last (Revelation 1:17), and the omnipotent Judge, Jury, and Executioner (Revelation 1:18).

How do these scriptures depict Him as being the first and the last, and the omnipotent Judge, Jury, and Executioner? Let's trek along with scriptural support of this metaphorical revelation of Jesus (Revelation 1:14-15), which uses symbolic features (hair, eyes, feet, and voice) to describe His persona, and for complementing the events taking place throughout the book of Revelation.

Revelation 1:14 focuses on His hair and eyes, "His head and his hair were white as white wool, like snow. His eyes were like a flame of fire." His hair being white identifies Him as being "Ancient of Days" (as depicted in Daniel 7:9) and full of wisdom. His eyes being like fire identifies Him as the omnipotent Judge, Jury, and Executioner as illustrated in Revelation 2:18-23 where He is readying to deal with the sin of Thyatira.

Revelation 1:15 focuses on His eyes and feet: "His feet were like burnished brass, as if it had been refined in a furnace. His voice was like the voice of many waters." His feet being like burnished brass symbolizes His righteous and sovereign authority, as exercised in Revelation 2:18. Throughout many biblical scriptures, whenever brass is mentioned, it signifies something that has been put through the fire and tested for durability, strength, and judgment. A prime example occurs in Number 21:9, when Moses crafts a serpent out of brass for those who were bitten by serpents because of their sins, to look upon for healing – an indiscreet foretelling of Christ being on the cross taking on the judgement for our sin. His voice having the sound like many waters represents the power and authoritativeness of His speaking, as depicted in Ezekiel 43:2, and in Genesis chapters 1 and 2, where He declared "Let there be..." during the creation of all there is.

Realizing these points regarding the description provided of Jesus in Revelation 1 will help in making sense of events in the succeeding chapters of Revelation. Also, they make good reference points when reading and connecting the Old Testament Christophanies with the incarnated New Testament Jesus.

Personification State

What are the significances of the seven angels and the seven churches (Revelation 1:20)?

Clearly, what the seven angels and the seven churches each represent is provided in Revelation 1:20. However, what many may not be aware of is the significance of the number seven and how the use of it translates to what is taking place throughout the book of Revelation. The number seven holds the symbolic meaning of "completeness" and "perfection." On the seventh day, God rested from all He created (Genesis 2:2); David describing the flawlessness of God's words as though purified seven times (Psalm 12:6); and Isaiah prophesying the coming of Jesus with Him embodying seven qualities (Isaiah 11:1-2). These all serve as usages of the number seven signifying either completeness and/or perfection.

Taking this information into account, we can surmise that the seven angels are the Spirit of God overseeing and at work throughout the body of Christ (i.e., the seven churches). How are the seven churches symbolic of the one body of Christ? 1 Corinthians 12:12-27 provides the blueprint of how we are all one body, interconnected and affecting one another. We (as believers) are all representing Christ, regardless of denomination, race, creed, color, language, etc. So, why is the number seven distinctly used here in Revelation 1:20? Although we are one body and governed by the Spirit of God, there are various adjustments that have been plaguing the church as a whole and as individual members, that need to be appropriately addressed. Each church within the body and its state of wellness requires a progress report and/or a tune up in order for the body to fully and properly function, according to the manufacturer's (God's) plan and purpose.

In order to help provide a clearer picture, as you look at the seven angels representing the perfect Spirit of God, liken this to both parents being on the same page, as one (a somewhat perfect union). Although each parent addresses different issues with the children, they both represent and operate as one. The same goes for the seven churches representing one body in Christ. Liken it to each child being a "Jones" family member (son or daughter), but also always representing the family as a whole (regardless of differences in age, grade, gender, and physical attributes). One child may be doing great and needs little or no assistance when in public, whereas others may require some discipline, direction, special attention, etc.

REVELATION 2

Overview

This chapter is the start of Jesus' messages to the first four of the seven churches (found in chapters two and three). His Spirit is introduced and manifested in seven forms with a focus on the condition of each of the seven churches (loveless, persecuted, compromising, corrupt, dead, faithful, and lukewarm). For each church, Jesus presents a summary of their statuses (addressing strengths and rebuking offenses) followed by encouraging words in the way of righteousness. A repetitive but most significant phrase found at the end of each letter to the churches is "He who overcomes." The Greek word for "overcome" is "nikao" and it means "to prevail" or "to conquer". It carries the connotation of not only withstanding an offense or an adversary but to prevail by not being conformed to its/their ways and/or ideologies, and most importantly, to prevail by repenting (turning from one's way). When reading these messages to the churches, understand that neither is a "one message fits all." In other words, the churches aren't established to mimic one another, but all are to represent Him in various degrees as a complement to one another – one body, many parts (1 Corinthians 12:12). Here are the discoveries to be addressed from among these first four churches:

Church of Ephesus (The Loveless Church)
1) What is the significance of Jesus' introduction to the church of Ephesus?
2) How did those of the church of Ephesus leave their first love?
3) What does the imposed penalty of moving the lampstand signify?
4) What are the works of the Nicolaitans?
5) What is meant by "I will give to eat from the tree of life?"

Church of Smyrna (The Persecuted Church)
1) What is the significance of Jesus' introduction to the church of Smyrna?
2) What is the significance of "the devil is about to throw some of you into prison, that you may be tested; and you will have oppression for ten days"?
3) What is the "crown of life"?
4) What is meant by "He who overcomes won't be harmed by the second death."?

Church of Pergamum (The Compromising Church)
1) What is the significance of Jesus' introduction to the church of Pergamum?
2) What's compromising about allowing the teachings of Balaam and the Nicolaitans?
3) What is meant by "I will make war against them with the sword of my mouth"?
4) What is "the hidden manna"?
5) What is the significance of having "a white stone with a new name written which no one knows but he who receives it"?

Church of Thyatira (The Corrupt Church)
1) What is the significance of Jesus' introduction to the church of Thyatira?
2) What is the significance of Jezebel (the prophetess) being in the church? (signifies accepting things done out of order

and without decency / accepting the messages of other religions such as karma, manifestation, name-it and claim-it, etc.)

3) What is meant by "I will kill her children with Death"?
4) What is "the morning star" to be given?

Scriptural Reading

[1]"To the angel of the assembly in Ephesus write:
"He who holds the seven stars in his right hand, he who walks among the seven golden lamp stands says these things:
[2]"I know your works, and your toil and perseverance, and that you can't tolerate evil men, and have tested those who call themselves apostles, and they are not, and found them false. [3]You have perseverance and have endured for my name's sake, and have not grown weary. [4]But I have this against you, that you left your first love. [5]Remember therefore from where you have fallen, and repent and do the first works; or else I am coming to you swiftly, and will move your lamp stand out of its place, unless you repent. [6]But this you have, that you hate the works of the Nicolaitans, which I also hate. [7]He who has an ear, let him hear what the Spirit says to the assemblies. To him who overcomes I will give to eat from the tree of life, which is in the Paradise of my God.
[8]"To the angel of the assembly in Smyrna write:
"The first and the last, who was dead, and has come to life says these things:
[9]"I know your works, oppression, and your poverty (but you are rich), and the blasphemy of those who say they are Jews, and they are not, but are a synagogue of Satan. [10]Don't be afraid of the things which you are about to suffer. Behold, the devil is about to throw some of you into prison, that you may be tested; and you will have oppression for ten days. Be faithful to death, and I will give you the crown of life. [11]He who has an ear, let him hear what the Spirit says to the assemblies. He who overcomes won't be harmed by the second death.
[12]"To the angel of the assembly in Pergamum write:

"He who has the sharp two-edged sword says these things:
¹³"I know your works and where you dwell, where Satan's throne is. You hold firmly to my name, and didn't deny my faith in the days of Antipas my witness, my faithful one, who was killed among you, where Satan dwells. ¹⁴But I have a few things against you, because you have there some who hold the teaching of Balaam, who taught Balak to throw a stumbling block before the children of Israel, to eat things sacrificed to idols, and to commit sexual immorality. ¹⁵So also you likewise have some who hold to the teaching of the Nicolaitans. ¹⁶Repent therefore, or else I am coming to you quickly and I will make war against them with the sword of my mouth. ¹⁷He who has an ear, let him hear what the Spirit says to the assemblies. To him who overcomes, to him I will give of the hidden manna, and I will give him a white stone, and on the stone a new name written which no one knows but he who receives it.

¹⁸"To the angel of the assembly in Thyatira write:

"The Son of God, who has his eyes like a flame of fire, and his feet are like burnished brass, says these things:
¹⁹"I know your works, your love, faith, service, patient endurance, and that your last works are more than the first. ²⁰But I have this against you, that you tolerate your woman Jezebel, who calls herself a prophetess. She teaches and seduces my servants to commit sexual immorality and to eat things sacrificed to idols. ²¹I gave her time to repent, but she refuses to repent of her sexual immorality. ²²Behold, I will throw her and those who commit adultery with her into a bed of great oppression, unless they repent of her works. ²³I will kill her children with Death, and all the assemblies will know that I am he who searches the minds and hearts. I will give to each one of you according to your deeds. ²⁴But to you I say, to the rest who are in Thyatira—as many as don't have this teaching, who don't know what some call 'the deep things of Satan'—to you I say, I am not putting any other burden on you. ²⁵Nevertheless, hold that which you have firmly until I come. ²⁶He who overcomes, and he who keeps my works to the end,

116

to him I will give authority over the nations. [27]He will rule them with a rod of iron, shattering them like clay pots, as I also have received of my Father; [28]and I will give him the morning star. [29]He who has an ear, let him hear what the Spirit says to the assemblies.

Questions & Discovery

Church of Ephesus (The Loveless Church)

What is the significance of Jesus' introduction to the church of Ephesus (Revelation 2:1)?

Revelation 1:20 provided the symbolic transliteration of the seven stars and seven golden lamp stands as representing the perfect Spirit of God and the church (body) of Christ. The salutatory introduction of Jesus to the church of Ephesus illustrates Him as the possessor of the (perfect) Spirit in righteousness (signified by being in His right hand) which actively and thoroughly inspects the church. The reason behind the inspection is because of love being noticeably missing and/or it having been replaced by legalism. This introduction serves as a reminder of being ready by not only knowing and performing the assignment given, but doing so by His Spirit of power, and of love, and of a sound mind (2 Timothy 1:7).

There are those of us who fit into this church and require this message because we employ an overly legalistic approach regarding Christianity. In all we do, godly love is to be exercised towards God and others (1 Corinthians 16:14).

How did those of the church of Ephesus leave their first love (Revelation 2:4)?

Leaving their first love required a movement in the opposite direction. This was the case for those of the church of Ephesus. Their first love of God remained stationary as they moved toward idealistic views of holiness through legalism. This is exactly what Jesus admonished and warned the scribes and Pharisees against doing in

Matthew 23. Later in scriptures, we find Paul reaffirming the need for love as part of our character and being evident in all we do (1 Corinthians 13:1-13); whereas John further endorses the case for the importance of love in action (1 John 4:7-8).

Leaving our first love occurs when our attention is taken off the work He is doing within us according to His will, and our eyes are fixed in pride on whatever work we're doing "for" Him based on our will and timing. Without the key ingredient of love, our compassion for others and godly passion for building the church declines as our pride and ego are bolstered.

What does the imposed penalty of moving the lampstand signify (Revelation 2:5)?

God moving their lampstand signifies them being repositioned out of an effective place of His favor and/or honor as illustrated in John 15:1-7. When a lampstand is moved (repositioned), people will no longer be able to see God but mere men working as gods. The salted flavor (i.e., words) of who they say they are becomes a bland and loveless, ineffective message (Matthew 5:13). In other words, when the lampstand is moved, one's light (testimony) that should present the love of God and Jesus as the way, becomes a showman's spotlight focused on man's embittered works and ambitions. We can only shine and share the light we have when we're plugged into His love (John 15:8-9).

What are the works of the Nicolaitans (Revelation 2:6)?

There is little known about exactly what the Nicolaitans were doing that the church of Ephesus and Jesus hated. However, what we do know is that God hates false worship and immorality. Apparently, the false worship of the Nicolaitans came in the form of what they were teaching, as stated in Revelation 2:15. In Revelation 2:2, we can find Jesus commending the church of Ephesus for not putting up with false teachings, and for having tested those found to be false apostles. This supports the offense of the Nicolaitans as being heretics. In Galatians 1:6-9, Paul addressed the issue of the spreading of heresy and pronounced a curse on anyone who teaches such. In 2 Peter 2, we're provided a stark description and warning of false teachers and their immoral ways. We have presented before us daily the message of good news (the Bible and a relationship with God) to nourish us spiritually, and a message of works which pleases the natural man (Galatians 5:17). One message prepares us for eternal life with God, and the other prepares us for eternal life separate from God.

What is meant by "I will give to eat from the tree of life (Revelation 2:7)?"

The blessing of having a right to eat from the tree of life signifies being accepted by God in righteousness (oneness of love in Christ). The promise of eating from the tree of life in Revelation 2:7 represents the totality of our needs being exceedingly met as we forever experience unimaginable bliss, glory, peace, and wellness in Him. Revelation 22:2 paints the picture of the tree of life yielding 12 kinds of fruit (one for each month in time as we know it), with the leaves being used for the healing of nations. In essence, every month (in a manner of speaking) we'll have new levels of utopia experiences in and with God eternally in the new heaven and earth (Revelation 21:1, Isaiah 66:22, and Isaiah 65:17). We shall be intricately in oneness with the heart of God, just as it was intended during the time of Adam and Even in the garden of Eden.

Church of Smyrna (The Persecuted Church)

What is the significance of Jesus' introduction to the church of Smyrna (Revelation 2:8)?

The salutatory introduction of Jesus to the church of Smyrna depicts Him as an encourager just as He presented Himself to the Apostle John (Revelation 1:8, 17 and 18). The reason for Him presenting Himself as an encourager is that believers are seemingly unable to "get ahead" in this world because of and despite having a lifestyle committed to serving God. Like then, the same occurs today. We are constantly bombarded with the problems of this world, the increasing lack of reverence for God, and the growing number of those who blasphemously proclaim to be believers but are not (as evidenced by their contradictory lifestyles).

In John 16, as Jesus was nearing His time of being crucified, He sensed the sadness and discouragement of His disciples. Therefore, He saw fit to encourage them not to lose heart (John 16:33). He didn't want them to recognize His purpose as a failure of hope nor as a defeat by the enemy. He needed them to comprehend and know the end result – His resurrection for our reconciliation. It's the same message delivered in His salutation to the church of Smyrna, as He reminds us to acknowledge Him as the first and the last, the Alpha and Omega, He who was dead but is now alive forevermore. Because He lives, not only do we live, but His Spirit is alive and living in us with the same power, helping us endure any and all that we encounter (Romans 8:11).

Yes, evil seems rampant about us and evildoers appear to be flourishing. However, our eyes mustn't be set on the physical aspect of what we see, but on the spiritual reality of who God is – our Source (1 Corinthians 8:6) and our Rewarder (Hebrews 11:6). He's fully aware of what's going on in the world and will deal with those issues at His timing. In the meantime, He's providing us daily doses of encouragement so that we do not lose heart, hope, or faith – becoming part of the problem rather than living as testimonial solutions.

What is the significance of "the devil is about to throw some of you into prison, that you may be tested; and you will have oppression for ten days"(Revelation 2:10)?

For most of us, when we hear the word prison, we understand it as being a place for someone who has broken a law. In the natural, there are various types of prisons meant to incarcerate lawbreakers based on age and/or degree of offense(s). There are juvenile detention centers, local jails, county jails, state penitentiaries, federal penitentiaries, etc. How Satan imprisons us in the spiritual sense is through the works of the flesh as mentioned in Galatians 5:19-21 and 1 Peter 4:3. He entices us to do something in the flesh that offends the holiness of God. Each of the mentioned works of the flesh are sins designed to keep us on lockdown, separated from God, and separated from purpose. Some receive short-term sentences, whereas others receive long-term sentences, but the effects of all are far reaching beyond just us (the offender). The only difference between the natural prisons and spiritual ones is that Satan doesn't discriminate – everyone's fair game with him.

So, how do these things relate to the believers who are a part of the church of Smyrna (the persecuted church) being thrown into prison and having oppression for ten days? The devil has, can, and will throw some of us into prison by either seducing us into becoming active participants and/or addicts to works of the flesh, or he can surround us with family, friends or communities who are indulging in such behaviors, which vexes our minds, souls, and spirits – imprisoning us in seemingly helpless and hopeless situations and affecting and testing our loyalty to God. Ultimately, he (the devil) would like nothing more than to destroy our testimony and us. The key to understanding the ten days of oppression that are mentioned is found in the number "10". Biblically, the number 10 signifies divine completion which, in this case, translates to the devil only being able to imprison us for a limited amount of time as authorized by God (Job 1:9-12 and 1 Cor 10:13).

There may be times when we're oppressed by the troubles about us and affecting us. However, we're not to mimic nor embrace them as the norm. We're to be encouraged by knowing Who we know and understanding that the troubles we see and/or experience today won't always be (Psalm 30:5). We're products of the God of hope and serve as His children - instruments to refocus the eyes and ears of a dying world by sharing His good news in how we live, speak, and think.

What is the "crown of life" (Revelation 2:10)?

As most of us are aware, whenever someone is seen wearing a crown, it hints at a certain level of royalty, importance, achievement, and/or wealth. Guess what? Here in Revelation 2:10, that same perception and distinctiveness applies, and it is truth as appointed, anointed, and promised by the word of God to these believers of the church of Smyrna (the persecuted). Take note of what Jesus says in the first portion of Revelation 2:9, "I know your works, oppression, and your poverty (**but you are rich**)…". Although it is not evident in this natural life as we know it, it is a revealed promise for the life to come. First Peter 2:9, encourages us believers to remember who we are in the spiritual, "…a chosen people, a royal priesthood…". In general, when we as human beings know something for certain, we tend to adjust to the truth of it in our lifestyle. Unfortunately, there are many of us who accept the truth of this world and are easily bought for a price of acceptance among the VIPs of this world. We sell out to debt by branding and adorning ourselves with the latest fashions, medically altering our physical appearances, and putting more trust and time in investing for this life with little concern for the life to come, let alone having a heart of compassion for the lost.

The crown of life spoken of here isn't attainable by our network connections among the rich and famous, nor the "wannabes". The crown of life Jesus is readying to present comes as an inheritance directly from Him, the King of kings. The crown of life that He will bestow on those who endure and are faithful is an actual incorruptible crown (1 Corinthians 9:25) depicting a prominent position of authority (2 Timothy 4:8), which will be worn during the eternal life to come. It's a crown that each will wear as they are set in positions of authority within kingdoms in the realms of the new heavens and earth. It's a crown that symbolizes tried and tested loyalty to God with unwavering faith.

What is meant by "He who overcomes won't be harmed by the second death" (Revelation 2:11)?

The first death was orchestrated and ushered in by the devil the moment Adam sinned (Romans 5:12). It not only produced expirations on mankind's biological existence by way of injecting us with sinful natures; it also produced a barrier in the relationship between God and mankind. The first death is something every human being is subject to experience in the physical at some point, including Enoch and Elijah as depicted in Revelation 11:3-12. For those who may not know, Enoch and Elijah are the only two righteous individuals taken alive by God (Genesis 5:24 / 2 Kings 2:1-11).

The second death is found in Revelation 20:14-15 and 21:8 and is identified as the lake of fire which is reserved for consuming God-rejecting beings (i.e., Satan, fallen angels (Jude 1:6), and mankind) who were found in the first death and constrained in hell. For those who are found in Christ and names are written in the Lamb's book of life (Revelation 21:27), they will in no way take part in the second death.

Church of Pergamum (The Compromising Church)

What is the significance of Jesus' introduction to the church of Pergamum (Revelation 2:12)?

The salutatory introduction of Jesus to the church of Pergamum portrays Him as Judge (same as described in Revelation 1:16) set against those who compromise by allowing and accepting teachings that are contrary to His word and negatively affecting their lifestyles and testimonies of Christ, although they uphold His name and faith. The same are those of us who proclaim Christ yet live, talk, react, and think like the world around us, not realizing that a "…little leaven leavens the entire lump…" (Galatians 5:9).

How does He present Himself as Judge before us today? In John 16:8, speaking of the role of the Holy Spirit, Jesus states, "When he has come, he will convict the world about sin, about righteousness, and about judgment." When we're walking in lockstep with the Holy Spirit, we are sensitive to spiritual convictions and nudges (i.e., intuitions) when something is off-kilter. Furthermore, we're to consult with His Spirit in testing and discerning what message is of God and what message isn't, according to 1 John 4:1-3. We do so by spending time in His word and allowing the Holy Spirit to speak to us regarding the situation at hand and/or verifying whether what is being said or taught matches up with what is written within the Word of God (i.e, the Bible).

What's compromising about allowing the teachings of Balaam and the Nicolaitans (Revelation 2:14-15)?

The teachings of Balaam and Nicolaitans are false teachings which water down the truth and promote the desires of the flesh. It's like mixing oil and water – it doesn't work and only creates confusion – and we know that God is not the author of confusion (1 Corinthians 14:33). In Matthew 6:24, Jesus affirms that no one can serve two masters (in this case it would be God and flesh).

The charge against Balaam was him teaching Balak how to entice the Israelites to sin by engaging in idolatry and sexual immorality, in hopes of the Israelites losing favor with God. Balaam knew that he couldn't pronounce a curse against the blessed Israelites, so instead, he provided another method to Balak, which was to appeal to their flesh (Numbers 24). As examined earlier within the church of Ephesus (Revelation 2:6), the Nicolaitans were proud false teachers of heresy and promoters of immorality. They convincingly used well-versed messages to promote their propaganda and dilute the effectiveness of God's word in the lives of whoever would listen; however, they primarily targeted believers.

The overall intent of such teachings is to disregard and/or eliminate God by promoting self-awareness campaigns that involve appeasing the lust of the flesh, lust of the eyes, and pride of life (1 John 2:16). Paul warns of these teachings in 2 Corinthians 11:3-4. These teachings are forbidden within God's church and must be addressed immediately when noticed. All too often, the church has allowed little pieces of information and practices to take place until it becomes very difficult to decipher the difference between the church and the world. It is a dangerously destructive compromise that causes many to stumble in their search for the way in Christ! This is why we need the Holy Spirit in the role of Judge to convict and guide us in righteousness.

What is meant by "I will make war against them with the sword of my mouth" (Revelation 2:16)?

Ephesians 6:17 identifies the "sword" as being the "word of God". The Greek translation of "word" is "rhéma" which means "spoken word" or an "utterance". It now beckons the question of, "What is the spoken word of God?" The answer is found in John 1, where Jesus is described as the living Word of God who was in the beginning, was with God, and was God. In Him, all authority resides both in heaven and on earth (Matthew 28:18). That word [Jesus] exemplifies the way, the truth, and the life according to John 14:6. This is important to know because as He appears to the church of Pergamum as Judge, He comes with full authority of exercising justice in truth. Therefore, war is waged not only against the false teachers as the word goes forth in truth contradicting their false teachings, but it is also waged as a disciplinary tool against those believers who failed to repent by continuing to compromise.

The mouthpiece used in waging this war is to be each believer who remains steadfast in faith and in His name. This is not to say that we are to be disrespectfully abrasive and haphazardly, 'all over the place' wielding the word. Rather, it means that we're to be ready to boldly and respectfully give a response when confronted with anything contradictory to the word of God (1 Peter 3:15-17 and 2 Timothy 2:15). His truth is the reason, as mentioned in Luke 12:51, that He came to bring division. Not that it is His will that we be people who are divided and at odds with one another, but for the sake of truth being known and accepted by whosoever will unto their salvation. War is waged in and by the truth of His word and is only fought against by those who refuse truth and choose to battle to their own demise (Romans 1:28-32).

What is "the hidden manna" (Revelation 2:17)?

Many of us remember the story from Exodus 16 when the children of Israel were wandering in the wilderness and became weary and hungry. To satisfy their hunger pangs, God miraculously fed them with bread from heaven. With them not knowing exactly what it was, they took to calling it "manna" (Exodus 16:31), which in Hebrew translates to "What is it?". Deuteronomy 8:3, 16 and Psalm 78:24 identifies their hunger as the reason for them receiving this "manna" and God using it as a teachable moment to make it clear that man shall not live by bread alone but by every word that proceeds from the mouth of the Lord.

That word which proceeds from the mouth of the Lord is none other than Jesus (as aforementioned). It's in John 1:1 where Jesus is described as the Word and it's in John 6:35 where He declares, "I am the bread of life." He is the true "manna" that many see as a mystery but is clearly revealed to His saints (Colossians 1:24-26). Here in Revelation 2:17, as a promised reward to those who overcome (remain steadfast in faith and in His name, and turn from compromising), He will be the complete satisfaction to their spiritual hunger.

What is the significance of having "a white stone with a new name written which no one knows but he who receives it" (Revelation 2:17)?

The Greek word for "white" is "leukos" and it means "brilliant, bright", possibly translucent. The Greek word for "stone" is "psēphon" and it means "a small stone, a pebble", possibly signifying a diamond type of stone. Why is this information important to know? Well, the first ordained priests of God were Aaron and his sons (Exodus 28). Part of the specifically coordinated outfits they were to wear consisted of a breastplate of judgment (Exodus 28:15). Within that breastplate were a setting of 12 stones (ruby, topaz, beryl, turquoise, sapphire, emerald, jacinth, agate, amethyst, chrysolite, onyx, and jasper) and on each of the stones was a name inscribed representing each of the 12 tribes of Israel.

Fast forward to the New Testament; remember that not only are we made kings and priests in Christ (Revelation 1:6), as Gentile believers, we are also grafted in with the Hebrews, making us one in the same (Romans 11:17-24). With that knowledge, those who remain steadfast in faith and in Christ, turning from compromising, and being defenders of the faith, are to be rewarded with a stone and a new name – representing Him as priest. They will metaphorically have a white stone embedded upon their breastplates, translucent in nature, illustrating their hearts reflecting the purity of truth in Christ.

The new name written shall signify the One whom they represent as the untainted, grafted, chosen people of God, who respectfully, boldly, and rightly divide the word of truth (2 Timothy 2:15).

Church of Thyatira (The Corrupt Church)

What is the significance of Jesus' introduction to the church of Thyatira (Revelation 2:18)?

The fiery eyes of Jesus symbolize His fury, while His bronze feet indicate His righteous authority as judge and readiness for warfare. The warfare He's having to contend with is that of weeding out what doesn't belong, as it damages the church by usurping the word and principles of God through egregiously erroneous teachings, practices, and false worshipping of idols. It is the patience of the Thyatira church for what they allow to go unchecked which fuels the righteous anger of Jesus. This same righteous anger of Jesus was manifested in the natural for the similar reason of idolatry as depicted in Matthew 21:12-13.

      The church can only serve and function properly on behalf of God by respecting and maintaining an open line of communication with God via prayer (Isaiah 56:7). When the line of communication and/or representation between the church and God is hindered and the church doesn't recognize the "clog", a foreign odor is released over a period of time. As the stench reaches the nostrils of God, He is moved to dislodge whatever is causing the clog and stench by any means necessary. This is exactly what He had done in Leviticus 10:1 when Nadab and Abihu (the sons of Aaron) offered strange fire, which is akin to our offering strange prayer (being mingled with false teachings, practices and worshipping of idols).

What is the significance of Jezebel (the prophetess) being in the church (Revelation 2:20)?

The name "Jezebel" in Hebrew is derived from "'ēze ba'al" and means, "Where is the Lord?", implying that the Lord doesn't really exist and/or the Lord is whoever or whatever you make him to be.

Jezebel is known as the manipulatively persuasive wife of Ahab (king of Israel). She was of Sidonian decent, and a devoted worshipper of the false god called "Ba'al". In Exodus 34:13-16, God prohibited the children of Israel from intermingled marriages with foreigners, warning that they would be led to worshipping false gods, sexual immorality, and eating things offered to idols. Ahab, disregarding God's warning against intermingled marriages, proceeded in marrying Jezebel (1 Kings 16:31), which opened the door in a mighty way for his offenses against God, the killing of God's servants and prophets (2 Kings 9:7), and his wicked leadership over the people of Israel (1 Kings 21:25-26).

What the spirit of Jezebel does is use manipulative words and/or acts to little-by-little creep in, usurp authority and take control as a god over one's mind, speech, and actions – exalting false gods and false narratives while diminishing and extinguishing worship and anything else that's tied to or represents the one true God. In short, the spirit of Jezebel is a form of witchcraft which aims to distort the truth and/or create confusion about truth by mingling it with deceptive lies that appease the eyes, flesh, and pride of its prey. This spirit of Jezebel as a prophetess promotes what pleases self and/or skillfully misuses the concepts of love (for accepting any and everything outside the word of God) and hate (for discrediting and disregarding any and everything within the word of God). Beware of those who are supposedly called to ministry within the church and use phrases such as, "If you love me…" or "Follow your heart…" etc. A true prophet or prophetess speaks only what saith the Lord (Deuteronomy 18:18).

For the record, yes, women can be called/used as prophetesses: Miriam (Exodus 15:20), Deborah (Judges 4:4), Huldah (2 Kings 22:14; 2 Chronicles 34:22), wife of Isaiah (Isaiah 8:3), Anna (Luke 2:36-38, and the four daughters of Philip (Acts 21:8-9). However, as 1 Corinthians 14:40 states, "Let all things be done decently and in order", not manipulatively with ulterior motives.

What is meant by "I will kill her children with Death"(Revelation 2:23)?

When speaking of Jezebel as the prophetess (Revelation 2:20), it is referring to the manipulative nature and spirit associated with Jezebel (as mentioned in 1 Kings 16:31) that has been passed along and is present within Thyatira types of churches. The implication of killing her (Jezebel's) children with death depicts a figurative result of what is to come for those who continue in the way of Jezebel. Killing them with death is the Lord completely cutting them off from existence. He (Jesus) is the One who has the keys of hades and of death, according to Revelation 1:18. It is He who can put an ultimate end to those who refuse to repent as they continue spreading and promoting false narratives under the guise of Christianity, all the while rejecting His truth and taking His mercy for granted.

What is "the morning star" to be given (Revelation 2:28)?

In Isaiah 14:12, the king of Babylonia (whom many believe to be in reference to Satan) is called the morning star. The term morning star symbolizes one who's shining, in excellence, or spotless. The Greek word for "I will give" is "dōsō" and it means "to put" or "set in place." In Revelation 22:16, Jesus identifies Himself as the Bright and Morning Star. The morning star that is to be given to those who overcome within the church of Thyatira is not a literal star that will be provided. Rather, it is a set position in the body of Christ (an extension of Him) which means they shall reflect and radiate His glorious nature. In 2 Peter 1:19, the Apostle Peter encourages believers to be steadfast in faith, for there will be a day when the morning star rises in our hearts. That morning star is the purity and excellence of Him (Jesus), whom the Thyatira overcomers will be able to richly share in.

REVELATION 3

Overview

As a continuation of Jesus' messages to the churches from chapter two, this chapter picks up at the fifth church and concludes with the seventh. The same format is followed in that Jesus presents a brief summary of their statuses (addressing strengths and rebuking offenses) along with encouraging words in the way of repentance and righteousness. As a reminder, when reading these messages to the churches, understand that neither is a "one message fits all." Here are the discoveries to be addressed regarding the final three churches:

Church of Sardis (The Dead Church)
1) What is the significance of Jesus' introduction to the church of Sardis?
2) Why are their works not found perfect?
3) What is the significance of having defiled garments?
4) What does the confessing of one's name before the Father and His angels signify?

Church of Philadelphia (The Faithful Church)
1) What is the significance of Jesus' introduction to the church of Philadelphia?

2) What does it mean to have "those of the synagogue of Satan" to "worship before your feet"?
3) What is the "hour of testing (trial)" that will come upon the entire world?
4) What does it mean to be a "pillar" in the temple of God?
5) What are the significances of the three names to be written on him who overcomes?

Church of the Laodiceans (The Lukewarm Church)
1) What is the significance of Jesus' introduction to the church of the Laodiceans?
2) What does "lukewarm" signify?
3) Explain Revelation 3:17-18?
4) What is the significance of hearing Jesus' voice and opening the door?

Scriptural Reading

[1]"And to the angel of the assembly in Sardis write:
"He who has the seven Spirits of God and the seven stars says these things:
"I know your works, that you have a reputation of being alive, but you are dead. [2]Wake up and strengthen the things that remain, which you were about to throw away, for I have found no works of yours perfected before my God. [3]Remember therefore how you have received and heard. Keep it and repent. If therefore you won't watch, I will come as a thief, and you won't know what hour I will come upon you. [4]Nevertheless you have a few names in Sardis that didn't defile their garments. They will walk with me in white, for they are worthy. [5]He who overcomes will be arrayed in white garments, and I will in no way blot his name out of the book of life, and I will confess his name before my Father, and before his angels. [6]He who has an ear, let him hear what the Spirit says to the assemblies.
[7]"To the angel of the assembly in Philadelphia write:

"He who is holy, He who is true, He who has the key of David, He who opens and no one can shut, and who shuts and no one opens, says these things:
[8]"I know your works (behold, I have set before you an open door, which no one can shut), that you have a little power, and kept My word, and didn't deny My name. [9]Behold, I make some of the synagogue of Satan, of those who say they are Jews, and they are not, but lie—behold, I will make them to come and worship before your feet, and to know that I have loved you. [10]Because you kept My command to endure, I also will keep you from the hour of testing which is to come on the whole world, to test those who dwell on the earth. [11]I am coming quickly! Hold firmly that which you have, so that no one takes your crown. [12]He who overcomes, I will make him a pillar in the temple of my God, and he will go out from there no more. I will write on him the name of My God and the name of the city of My God, the new Jerusalem, which comes down out of heaven from My God, and My own new name. [13]He who has an ear, let him hear what the Spirit says to the assemblies.
[14]"To the angel of the assembly in Laodicea write:
"The Amen, the Faithful and True Witness, the Beginning of God's creation, says these things:
[15]"I know your works, that you are neither cold nor hot. I wish you were cold or hot. [16]So, because you are lukewarm, and neither hot nor cold, I will vomit you out of my mouth. [17]Because you say, 'I am rich, and have gotten riches, and have need of nothing,' and don't know that you are the wretched one, miserable, poor, blind, and naked; [18]I counsel you to buy from me gold refined by fire, that you may become rich; and white garments, that you may clothe yourself, and that the shame of your nakedness may not be revealed; and eye salve to anoint your eyes, that you may see. [19]As many as I love, I reprove and chasten. Be zealous therefore, and repent. [20]Behold, I stand at the door and knock. If anyone hears my voice and opens the door, then I will come in to him and will dine with him, and he with me. [21]He who overcomes, I will give to him to sit down with me on my throne, as I also overcame and sat down with

my Father on his throne. ²²He who has an ear, let him hear what the Spirit says to the assemblies."

Questions & Discovery

Church of Sardis (The Dead Church)

What is the significance of Jesus' introduction to the church of Sardis (Revelation 3:1)?

This is an introduction to remind the church of Sardis who He is in the sense of being omnipotent, omniscient and omnipresent. Letting them know that He is alive and witnessing all things (Hebrews 4:13), whether commendable or lamentable. This dead church (Sardis) represents those who merely have an appearance or reputation of godliness or holiness with little to no work (i.e., lifestyle) that complements or affirms them having a relationship with God. These are those who exhibit a show of faith without works (i.e., lifestyle) as identified in James 2:14-26.

Why are their works not found perfect (Revelation 3:2)?

Their works were missing the key ingredients of having a lifestyle exemplifying their supposed faith and having a sincere reverence for God. What the church of Sardis lacks is a true relationship with God, very similar to the Pharisees being full of dead men's bones (Matthew 23:27); but they go a step further by neglecting the use of their giftings and talents toward building God's kingdom. They are more akin to the servant who received one talent and did nothing with it (Matthew 25:14-29). Or better yet, their works were not found perfect because they found life in worldly dead things (i.e., names/titles, material riches, etc.) rather than the work they first committed themselves to – leaving the kingdom's business unfinished and left to suffer.

Jesus not finding their works perfect is an exact illustration of Cain's offering to God being found unacceptable (Genesis 4:5-16). The picture of how they see themselves in no way reflects the image of having a relationship with God (James 1:23-27). One's lifestyle (personality, conduct, and belief system) reveals who or what they serve.

What is the significance of having defiled garments (Revelation 3:4)?

The symbolization of having defiled garments depicts being covered/bonded in a lifestyle of depravity (Zechariah 3:3-4). In the case with those of the church of Sardis, they appear to be consumed in immoral living to the point of not realizing they are in such a state. In essence, they have become accustomed to living roguishly. Jesus makes this known to them with His Spirit of conviction, as a show of mercy, before they're turned over to having reprobate minds.

What does the confessing of one's name before the Father and His angels signify (Revelation 3:5)?

Jesus confessing one's name before the Father and His angels signifies that He knows and vouches for you (Matthew 10:32). He is the gatekeeper and pass granter for all who possess a relationship with Him. He grants us this favor as we live out our faith introducing others to Him by how we exercise and execute the fruit of the Holy Spirit as identified in Galatians 5:22-26. Our confession of Him is evident by our love and faith in Him, shown in how we live and interact with those around us.

To have Jesus confess our names before the Father and His angels pulls us into His family, giving us the right to boldly come before the throne of our gracious God (Hebrews 4:16). As we come before Him in prayer, we know that He dependably hears and answers our petitions according to His will (1 John 5:14-15). We are afforded the same rights as Jesus (with us being the body of Jesus – the church) with the Father and His angels. Likewise, when we have a relationship with Jesus, not only are we able to confess His name to others, but He also gains access to all that we are as His Spirit is housed within us. His Spirit acts as the Counselor for teaching, guiding, and reminding us of Jesus as the Son of God, Word of God, etc. (John 14:26).

Church of Philadelphia (The Faithful Church)

What is the significance of Jesus' introduction to the church of Philadelphia (Revelation 3:7)?

The term "Philadelphia" derives from the conjoined Greek words "phílos" meaning "loving friend" and "adelphiós" meaning "a brother". It's where the United States' city of Philadelphia gets the moniker of the "City of Brotherly Love" – a name and moniker first bestowed upon and given in recognition of this church (Philadelphia) mentioned here in Revelation 3:7. In the salutation of Jesus to the church of Philadelphia, He affirms who they believe and respect Him to be based on their love for one another. This coincides with His commandment for believers to love one another (John 13:34) and appropriately illustrates love for God (1 John 4:20).

By having that true brotherly love for one another, they (church of Philadelphia) exemplify what He personifies – holiness and truth (1 Peter 1:16 and 1 John 5:20). They see Him as being on the throne, in full control (Matthew 19:28). They see Him possessing the keys to open and to shut doors of blessings, judgments, answers to petitions, etc. (Isaiah 22:22). They, too, possess the keys of the kingdom of heaven, to bind and loose (Matthew 16:19). They are a mirror image of Who He is and what He represents in love.

What does it mean to have "those of the synagogue of Satan" to "worship before your feet" (Revelation 3:9)?

There are those who attempt to mingle in and identify as believers based on immaculate appearances, prestigious orthodox language, and polished religious mannerisms, who are no more than deceitful workers of the devil (Satan), living lies. They are experts at seeking and receiving worship toward themselves, all the while discrediting true believers by making mockery of them and their godly peculiarity. Their job is to create confusion by transferring the pure word of God into works of penance, acting as spiritual fathers in place of the salvation offered in Jesus and mercy by the work He has finished. Though they may dare to publicly declare themselves as being of the synagogue (church) of Satan, the truth remains that they are. They set up for themselves temples and religious governments, claiming to be an order of the Jews by adopting Jewish customs and practices for the sake of power, prestige, and money. They see holiness in themselves but are only blinded by their prideful sin (Luke 18:11).

Those who are true believers in God face much persecution and challenges in sharing the good news of Jesus because of the confusion Christianity has become and the ever-present temptations. However, their endurance and the love they have for one another serves well in promoting and testifying of the one true God. There will be a day when those of the 'synagogue of Satan' will have to bow down before those who are in Christ and worship at the feet of Jesus (Isaiah 60:14, 45:23, Philippians 2:10-11, and Romans 14:11). This will come to pass as these groups of loyal believers will be revealed and identified as one in and with Christ during His return, with rewards and judgements presented (Revelation 20:11-15 and 22:12).

What is the "hour of testing (trial)" that will come upon the entire world (Revelation 3:10)?

The word "testing" is derived from the Greek word "peirasai" and it means "to try" with the connotation of proving someone, as to where they stand spiritually and/or what they are made of. In other words, there are many who require frequent testing in order to build what little faith they may have (Romans 10:17) or to mature the fruit of the spirit residing within (Galatians 5:22-23). Also, there are those churches requiring testing in order to weed out and detach those who pretentiously attach themselves to the church, being nothing more than blemishing hinderances for the growth, maturity, holiness, and focus of the church. However, those of the church of Philadelphia will not have to endure this "hour of testing" to prove who they are because their endurance and loyalty to God is proven by their lifestyle.

Now, this "hour of testing" is not a set 60-minute amount of time as we may think of. It's figuratively and literally speaking of a span of time being as long as it takes according to God's will and purpose; not only does it refer to testing with regard to what is faced in the present time of everyday life, but it also refers to the time immediately following the rapture of those of the church of Philadelphia (Revelation 3:10), a period known as the great tribulation, which is described and takes place in Revelation 6 through 19 within the seven-sealed scroll, sounding of seven trumpets, and three "woes" to come. The great tribulation (aka "hour of testing") is a period of God's longsuffering and merciful plea for people to know Him and a time in which the hate and rejection of God by mankind will manifest in them making martyrs of the people of God. It's during this period when the faith of the people of the churches of Smyrna, Sardis, Laodicea, Thyatira, Ephesus, and Pergamum will either prove themselves as belonging to God or as great pretenders.

Within the great tribulation period arises the antichrist (Revelation 13). During the reign of the antichrist, there will be tremendous trials like none of us have ever witnessed; it will be a time when one's life will literally be on the line, as having to pledge allegiance to the antichrist or face death for the sake of Christ. No need to tell you, but it's best to be in right standing with God now and follow in line with the church of Philadelphia believers. In Christ, we have the assurance that "…the Lord knows how to deliver the godly out of temptations and to reserve the unjust under punishment for the day of judgment" (2 Peter 2:9).

What does it mean to be a "pillar" in the temple of God (Revelation 3:12)?

The word "pillar" in the Greek is "stylon" and it denotes "pillar" or "support" – signifying having a sustained position in supporting what one believes. It's being at peace and as one with what it upholds – Jesus being the way, truth, and life (John 14:6). These figurative pillars are set in place by the builder (Jesus) and represent those who have been called and who have accepted His calling, such as James, Peter, and John (Galatians 2:9) as well as the other appointed Apostles. As a matter of fact, in John 14:2, He proclaims that in His Father's house there are many "mansions". The Greek term for "mansions" is "monai" and translates as "dwelling-place" or "much room" – meaning to be guaranteed permanent residence. To be a pillar in the temple of God is to be a sustained resident, heir of God and co-heir with Christ (Romans 8:17) for eternity. This is an honorable position reserved for those of the church of Philadelphia.

What are the significances of the three names to be written on him who overcomes (Revelation 3:12)?

Firstly, let's understand that whenever "three" is mentioned in the Bible, it signifies perfection and completeness as associated with God's power and presence. Just as the Father, Son, and Holy Spirit make up the Trinity (1 John 5:7), they also epitomize God's unified completeness, perfection, power, and presence. Therefore, the three names to be written on him who overcomes denotes being complete in the image of God as in the intended creation of Adam and Eve prior to their fall (Genesis 1:27). The writing of the three names on the overcomers (within the church of Philadelphia) is metaphorical with the implication of not only being symbolically tagged as God's property, but also seen as living exact likenesses/images of Him.

So, what is the significance of the three names to be written on him who overcomes (within the church of Philadelphia)? The first is the writing on him (overcomers within the church of Philadelphia) the name of His God. This shows being known by the fruit produced from a direct relationship with the Father and a readiness as a fiancée (Matthew 7:20, Romans 8:15, and Ephesians 5:26). The second is the writing on him (overcomers within the church of Philadelphia) the name of the city of His God. This implies being the bride of Christ (Revelation 21:2) and becoming one with Him in marriage (Isaiah 54:5). The final is the writing of Jesus' new name on him (overcomers within the church of Philadelphia). This signifies a figurative act of consummation which affirms ownership (2

Corinthians 1:22). By them having all three names metaphorically inscribed on them, they will then completely represent in righteousness and reign alongside Christ (Romans 5:17 and 2 Corinthians 5:17).

Church of The Laodiceans (The Lukewarm Church)

What is the significance of Jesus' introduction to the church of the Laodiceans (Revelation 3:14)?

The Greek word for "Laodicea" comes from the conjoined words of "laos" meaning "people" and "dike" meaning "justice" or "judgment". The proper translation of "Laodicea" is "the justice of the people." In His introduction to the church of the Laodiceans, Jesus acknowledges Himself as the Amen, the Faithful and True Witness, and the Beginning of God's creation. The Greek word for "Amen" is "amēn" and translates as "so be it", which presents Him as the final authority. The Greek word for "Faithful" is "pistos" and translates as "reliable"; the Greek word for "True" is "alēthinos" and translates as "made of truth"; and the Greek word for "Witness" is "martus" and translates as "testifier" with the connotation of being a martyr. Therefore, the title "the Faithful and True Witness" identifies Him as the reliable and true martyr. The Greek word for "Beginning" is "archē" and translates as "origin" or "source", which presents Him as the starting point of all God's creation.

The culmination of His significant titles in this introduction to the church of the Laodiceans not only serves as a reminder to the targeted audience but it vehemently reinforces Him as being the final authority, reliable and true martyr, and the source of all God's creation. The people of the church of the Laodiceans are those who forget or straddle the fence about who He is and who they represent. Although He is the justice of the people (Laodiceans), they seem to forget it and continue living life straddling the fence, seeing God as their source but depending on their material "blessings" as identifying their worth.

What does "lukewarm" signify (Revelation 3:16)?

The Greek word for "lukewarm" is "chliaros" and it means to be tepid. What is tepid? Tepid is having little enthusiasm, which (in the context of this verse) equates to giving God minimum time, talent, and resources – only communicating with Him or witnessing about Him at one's convenience or whenever a selfish need arises. Being lukewarm is being the type of person whose faith conveniently and occasionally match their lifestyle, making it difficult for anyone to differentiate if they're a believer or not. Simply put, it signifies having a lack of passion for God – mediocre interest. Romans 12:11 stirs up believers to "never be lacking in zeal, but keep your spiritual fervor, serving the Lord...", whereas 2 Peter 3:18 challenge believers to "...grow in the grace and knowledge of our Lord and Savior Jesus Christ." Believers aren't to be idle and should have more enthusiasm about the things of God than they had about the things of the world before being saved.

Explain Revelation 3:17-18.

The gist of Jesus' charge against the Laodiceans (Revelation 3:17-18) is them finding value of themselves based on the gainful accumulation of what this world identifies with as being rich (successful), all the while neglecting and/or rejecting God's spiritual food and development of being like Jesus. Their appetites for the word of God have been marred because of the appeasing of their flesh and the "glory" of their status in the world. Much like the rich young ruler who was seeking how to attain eternal life (Matthew 19:16-22) and instructed to part with his riches by taking care of the poor, he, too, found it to be a difficult thing to do. Instead, his excitement and willingness to have eternal life was quickly extinguished, as it goes on to say that he (the rich young ruler) heard what was required and went away sorrowful because he had many possessions.

Understand that God is not against anyone being rich. The problem arises when worldly riches define who we are at our heart's core, and sits on the throne of our hearts instead of God being there – God no longer has the priority. Matthew 6:33 underlines how we are to prioritize God's kingdom and righteousness above all else as it proclaims, "But seek first God's Kingdom and his righteousness; and all these things will be given to you as well." Isaiah 55:1-2 complements Revelation 3:17-18 as it states, "Hey! Come, everyone who thirsts, to the waters! Come, he who has no money, buy, and eat! Yes, come, buy wine and milk without money and without price. Why do you spend money for that which is not bread, and your labor for that which doesn't satisfy? Listen diligently to me, and eat that which is good, and let your soul delight itself in richness."

So, what is Jesus saying by his advising the Laodiceans to buy from Him gold refined by fire and white garments? As supported by Matthew 16:24, He's advising them to deny what they think of themselves by overcoming the desires of glorying in the flesh, according to what the world defines as self-worth, and to fully digest the word of God for their transformations to the likeness of Jesus (having all their needs met by God's riches) according to Ephesians 3:16. Those of the church of Laodicea would be served best by following the model of these wise words found in Hebrews 12:1-2:

"Therefore let's also, seeing we are surrounded by so great a cloud of witnesses, lay aside every weight and the sin which so easily entangles us, and let's run with perseverance the race that is set before us, looking to Jesus, the author and perfecter of faith, who for the joy that was set before him endured the cross, despising its shame, and has sat down at the right hand of the throne of God."

What is the significance of hearing Jesus' voice and opening the door (Revelation 3:20)?

Hearing the voice of Jesus requires spiritual sensitivity to His word, whether received by what is read, heard (whether intuitively or orally), or observed (be it surrounding nature or the lifestyle and conduct of other believers). The key to being spiritually aware of what He is saying lies within having a desire to know, a discipline to seek, and a humbleness to ask (pray). Romans 10:13-15 states:

"Whoever will call on the name of the Lord will be saved." How then will they call on him in whom they have not believed? How will they believe in him whom they have not heard? How will they hear without a preacher? And how will they preach unless they are sent? As it is written: "How beautiful are the feet of those who preach the Good News of peace, who bring glad tidings of good things!"

Hearing His voice is the beginning of greater to come. However, greater can't come if the door to the heart is closed. "Knowing is half the battle", cliché-ish but true. What is known, or better yet, when it is known that it is Jesus knocking on the door of the heart, the door must be opened for Him to enter in – this calls for those of the Laodicean church to humble themselves, let down their guard, and welcome Him in – surrendering to Him as Lord. Once He is welcomed in, He can begin the renovation process of dealing with the heart and mind. Those are the two major organs needing to be transformed in order for His word to be kept, His will to be carried out, and His Spirit to reside (John 14:23). Afterward, they move from being hearers to doers (James 1:22).

REVELATION 4

Overview

In this chapter, as John continues his extraordinary divinely spiritual journey, he is taken from witnessing the writing of the letters to the seven churches to a door located in heaven. As the door is opened and he is invited in to witness future events, he is greeted with a divinely majestic and mystique sight representing the throne space of God. In this holy utopian setting, he is only able to limitedly describe what is seen using his native terminology of adjectives – mostly metaphorical terms and phrases. The quintessence of what he observes is the categorical holiness of God sitting on the throne surrounded by sacred beings offering thanks, honor, and glory to Him nonstop. Beholding this eventful scene prepares John for what he would be shown concerning the future. It's only when God can be seen and received as Lord of lords and King of kings, that then one can clearly see what is to come, as Isaiah 6:1 attest. Discoveries to be addressed regarding this chapter are identified below:

1. Describe the difference in the Spirit speaking to John in Revelation 1:10 and Revelation 4:1.
2. Explain John being in the spirit and expound on God's appearance.

3. What is the significance of the twenty-four thrones and the twenty-four elders seated on those thrones?
4. What is the significance of the four living creatures being in the middle of the throne and around the throne?

Scriptural Reading

[1]After these things I looked and saw a door opened in heaven; and the first voice that I heard, like a trumpet speaking with me, was one saying, "Come up here, and I will show you the things which must happen after this."
[2]Immediately I was in the Spirit. Behold, there was a throne set in heaven, and one sitting on the throne [3]that looked like a jasper stone and a sardius. There was a rainbow around the throne, like an emerald to look at. [4]Around the throne were twenty-four thrones. On the thrones were twenty-four elders sitting, dressed in white garments, with crowns of gold on their heads. [5]Out of the throne proceed lightnings, sounds, and thunders. There were seven lamps of fire burning before his throne, which are the seven Spirits of God. [6]Before the throne was something like a sea of glass, similar to crystal. In the middle of the throne, and around the throne were four living creatures full of eyes before and behind. [7]The first creature was like a lion, the second creature like a calf, the third creature had a face like a man, and the fourth was like a flying eagle. [8]The four living creatures, each one of them having six wings, are full of eyes around and within. They have no rest day and night, saying, "Holy, holy, holy is the Lord God, the Almighty, who was and who is and who is to come!"
[9]When the living creatures give glory, honor, and thanks to him who sits on the throne, to him who lives forever and ever, [10]the twenty-four elders fall down before him who sits on the throne and worship him who lives forever and ever, and throw their crowns before the throne, saying, [11]"Worthy are you, our Lord and God, the Holy One, to receive the glory, the honor, and the power, for you created all things, and because of your desire they existed and were created!"

Questions & Discovery

The Spirit Speaks

Describe the difference in the Spirit speaking to John in Revelation 1:10 and Revelation 4:1.

Interestingly, the voice of the Spirit went from speaking behind John (Revelation 1:10) to speaking with him (Revelation 4:1). When the Spirit spoke to John from behind, it was introducing John to a metaphorical description of Jesus, with each part introducing His temperament toward each of the seven churches (Revelation 1:11-20). The Spirit speaking from behind provokes us by providing His guidance for us to act upon (Isaiah 30:21) as our responsibility. When speaking with John here in Revelation 4, the Spirit now invites him to come up, behind an open door in heaven, to be shown the future of what is to come after the churches have been addressed. The Spirit speaking with us readies us (in peace) for what is to come, whether good or bad, according to His will (Matthew 10:19-20, Luke 1:30-32, and Acts 9:10-19).

Wind and Wonderful

Explain John being in the spirit and expound on God's appearance (Revelation 4:2-3).

Here in Revelation 4:2, the Greek word for "spirit" is "pneúma" and it denotes "the wind". The statement of John being in the spirit can best be characterized as him being in the form of the wind, following the lead of God's (invisible) Spirit. For this literal transformation to occur, John's physical body was in a deep coma (if not completely dead, it was the closest to death as one can experience). As his body laid comatose, his undying spirit was sustained and guided by God's Spirit into the high heavens – witnessing what our natural eyes could not withstand nor behold.

In Revelation 4:2-3, John observes a throne and someone sitting on the throne. The one seen seated on the throne is God (Ezekiel 1:26) with emblematic appearances described as stones of jasper and sardius; however, keep in mind that the Father, Son, and Spirit are one (1 John 5:7). The Greek word for "jasper" is "iaspidi" and it refers to "a translucent stone"; and the Greek word for "sardius" is "sardion" and it refers to "a precious stone of divine splendor." Therefore, what John saw and described was the essence of the Father in translucent form, possessing a uniquely divine splendor/beauty. The rainbow he saw encapsulating the throne represents the illuminating glory of the Lord (Ezekiel 1:28), bearing resemblance to an emerald which most often symbolizes life (James 1:17-18). It attests to all life originating from Jesus (the living word of God).

24 Thrones, 24 Elders

What is the significance of the twenty-four thrones and the twenty-four elders seated on those thrones (Revelation 4:4)?

Let's start with the basics. Biblically, the number 12 represents completeness, authority and divine order as illustrated by the 12 tribes of Israel in Genesis 49:1-28 (divine connection), the 12 disciples of Jesus in Luke 6:12-13 (divine purpose), the 12 gates of Jerusalem in Revelation 21:12 (divine perfection), and the 12 stars in Revelation 12:1-2 (divine protection). Each grouping of 12 serves a distinct function in God's relationship with mankind, all the while signifying His position of headship (authority).

When the number 12 is doubled (to 24), it's now referring to our relationship toward God (in how we and all creation are to view Him in reverence, holiness, and worship). Biblically, the number 24 is associated with the priesthood and worship of God according to the responsibilities and order of the Levites and musicians (1 Chronicles 23 and 24). What they couldn't do perfectly and infinitely, He was and is – our King and High Priest. It symbolizes the perfect power and authority of God and coincides with the reign of Jesus as depicted by the 24 things He will do as King and Priest which are annotated in Psalm 72. The twenty-four thrones and twenty-four elders metaphorically illustrate His divine and sovereign Lordship.

Literally, the twenty-four thrones and twenty-four elders are those unidentified elect persons who represent all of mankind and all of heaven's celestial beings as pure in heart worshippers (kings and priests of worship) of the deserving Almighty God. There being 24 of them indicates a far higher degree (the ultimate degree) of honor, reverence and worship, which is rightly warranted for the one sitting on the throne (God). In the natural, this can be similar to special honors, pomp and circumstance protocols government officials receive based on their positions – e.g. the President would always receive higher honors and, practically, require double the honor guard personnel than a governor would. In the case mentioned here in Revelation 4, God receives and deserves the ultimate honors.

All-seeing

What is the significance of the four living creatures being in the middle of the throne and around the throne (Revelation 4:6-8)?

Here in Revelation 4:6-8, we're presented with extraordinary and unimaginable information regarding four living creatures, with eyes before and behind them, positioned in the middle of the throne and around the throne. Each of these living creatures maintains a unique symbolic resemblance: lion, calf, face of a man, and a flying eagle. They all have six wings, eyes inside and out, and repeatedly proclaim, "Holy, holy, holy is the Lord God, the Almighty, who was and who is and who is to come!" Ironically, these very same creatures bear a striking resemblance to those shown to the prophet Ezekiel as he is provided a vision of a windstorm exemplifying the presence of God and containing the glory of God along with four living creatures (Ezekiel 1).

So, what is the significance of these creatures? In essence, each creature speaks of God's character and are revealed to John in varying descriptive entities that correspond with Jesus' image as well as the magnitude of who God is. The lion denotes Jesus as the lion of Judah (Revelation 5:5) and indicates God's authority and power (Genesis 49:9); the calf represents Jesus as the perfect sacrifice (Hebrews 10:1-14) and the requirement of God's reconciliation plan (John 3:16); having the face of a man signifies Jesus as being the second and perfect Adam (1 Corinthians 15:45-49) and the righteous image of God (Genesis 1:27); and the eagle symbolizes God's protection and faithfulness (2 Thessalonians 3:3 and Psalm 91:4). All four creatures having six wings exemplifies the uniqueness of God being the One who is omnipresent, omnipotent, and omniscient – unmatched by anyone or anything. The creatures having eyes everywhere (full of eyes inside and out) symbolize His translucent holiness. He's tried and tested throughout and found to be without any blemish whatsoever that disqualifies Him from being on the throne. The proclamation they endlessly utter (Holy, Holy, Holy...) avows who He is in the purest of truth.

REVELATION 5

Overview

This chapter serves as the beginning of the time known as the "Day of the Lord" (1 Thessalonians 5:2) with the introduction of the "seven-sealed book." In Revelation 5:5-6, we find that Jesus is the only one worthy to open the book as He is presented as the Lamb, the Lion of the tribe of Judah, and the Root of David (all signifying His royal Kingship and Authority). In Revelation 5:11-12, we are provided a sneak preview of countless angels announcing Jesus as being worthy to receive power, riches, wisdom, strength, honor, glory, and blessing – demonstrating His exemplification of perfect worship and praise. Furthermore, in Revelation 5:13, every creature loudly proclaims blessing, honor, glory, and power to God (Father and Son, John 10:30), who sits on the throne. In this chapter, we'll discuss and examine the following:

1. Why was there no one able to open or look inside the book located in the right hand of God?
2. Who or what comprises every "created thing" worshipping God in Revelation 5:13?

Scriptural Reading

[1]I saw, in the right hand of him who sat on the throne, a book written inside and outside, sealed shut with seven seals. [2]I saw a mighty angel proclaiming with a loud voice, "Who is worthy to open the book, and to break its seals?" [3]No one in heaven above, or on the earth, or under the earth, was able to open the book or to look in it. [4]Then I wept much, because no one was found worthy to open the book or to look in it. [5]One of the elders said to me, "Don't weep. Behold, the Lion who is of the tribe of Judah, the Root of David, has overcome: he who opens the book and its seven seals."

[6]I saw in the middle of the throne and of the four living creatures, and in the middle of the elders, a Lamb standing, as though it had been slain, having seven horns and seven eyes, which are the seven Spirits of God, sent out into all the earth. [7]Then he came, and he took it out of the right hand of him who sat on the throne. [8]Now when he had taken the book, the four living creatures and the twenty-four elders fell down before the Lamb, each one having a harp, and golden bowls full of incense, which are the prayers of the saints. [9]They sang a new song, saying,

"You are worthy to take the book
and to open its seals,
for you were killed,
and bought us for God with your blood
out of every tribe, language, people, and nation,
[10]and made us kings and priests to our God;
and we will reign on the earth."

[11]I looked, and I heard something like a voice of many angels around the throne, the living creatures, and the elders. The number of them was ten thousands of ten thousands, and thousands of thousands, [12]saying with a loud voice, "Worthy is the Lamb who has been killed to receive the power, wealth, wisdom, strength, honor, glory, and blessing!"

[13]I heard every created thing which is in heaven, on the earth, under the earth, on the sea, and everything in them, saying, "To

him who sits on the throne and to the Lamb be the blessing, the honor, the glory, and the dominion, forever and ever! Amen!" [14]The four living creatures said, "Amen!" Then the elders fell down and worshiped.

Questions & Discovery

The Seven-Sealed Book

Why was there no one able to open or look inside the book located in the right hand of God besides the Lamb (Revelation 5:1-4)?

Let's first define the book and its purpose. The book John sees in the [symbolic] right hand of God [the Father] is of the likeness of the prophetic scroll provided to the prophet Ezekiel in Ezekiel 2. It had writings (inside and outside) consisting of lamentations (Hebrew: qînim – expressed passion or zeal (for rescuing the dead)), mourning (Hebrew: wāhegeh – expressed meditation, rumbling, moaning), and woes (Hebrew: wāhî – expressed sorrows and griefs). The same (lamentations, mourning, and woes) are found inside the book mentioned in Revelation 5 and illustrated by the seven seals, seven trumpets, and seven bowls found in Revelation 6-19.

Much like Ezekiel was sent to speak the prophetic word of God to the wayward and backslidden Hebrews (Ezekiel 2 and 3), such is the purpose of this written book found here in Revelation 5 for Christ to release on all nations for the sake of believers being redeemed. The purpose of the book serves as an extension of God's grace and mercy toward those who fall within six of the seven churches mentioned in Revelation 2 and 3 (remember those of the church of Philadelphia are exempt due to the rapture (Revelation 3:10)) as well as drawing unbelievers to becoming believers from outside the church. This corresponds with the loving kindness of His will that none should perish but all should come to repentance (2 Peter 3:9). The book holds the testing for weeding out believers from non-believers (Matthew 13:30) and God's final judgments on Satan and all those who follow after him and his ways.

Why is all that important? It is important because it supports why there was no one found (other than the Lamb) able to receive, open, and look inside the book. No one besides the Lamb was qualified. In essence, the book consists of penalties and judgments for all our sins – every offense which does not measure up to God's standard of holiness. This means that the only person who can delve out what's in this book must be a qualified official (without fault (sin)) and someone who cannot only relate to mankind's sin but who identifies with God's holiness. What qualifies Him to be worthy is His victory over sin and death (1 Corinthians 15:57), His resurrection, and being identified as the Son of God (Romans 1:4). He became our righteousness and puts us in right standing with the Father (2 Corinthians 5:1). After taking upon Himself our sin (Isaiah 53:5-6)) and defeating it, experiencing the Father forsaking Him momentarily because of Him bearing our sin (Mark 15:34), He was repositioned to being one with the Father (John 10:30). He was tried and tested, yet He prevailed in truth and is hailed as King. With Him being able to receive, open, and break the seven seals of the book, He is firmly established as being the way, the truth, and the life (John 14:6).

For believers, we're made holy by accepting Jesus as our sacrifice (Hebrews 10:10). However, because most believers contend with and succumb to corrupt habits of Christianity, those believers (found within the six churches) who are alive when the tribulation takes place will have to endure/overcome the tribulation by the cost of their lives to the glory of Christ (Revelation 6:11 and 20:4).

Acknowledge Him

Who or what comprises every "created thing" worshipping God in Revelation 5:13?

The assertive, straightforward answer would imply that all mankind makes up those worshipping God in Revelation 5:13. Yes, that would be simple; however, that is not the case. Revelation 20 sheds light on there being two resurrections taking place, one for believers and the other for non-believers. It's during the time of these resurrections when all mankind will surely fulfill the prophetic messages of Isaiah 45:23, Philippians 2:10, and Romans 14:11 with every knee bowing and every tongue confessing to God.

Here in Revelation 5:13, "created thing" is translated as "ktisma" in the Greek and it denotes things that were built and established in set places. In Romans 1:20, we know that creation (i.e., seas, stars, mountains, etc.) serves as evidence of God's power and divine nature, and testifies of His existence. Furthermore, in Romans 8:22-23, we read and understand that creation (i.e., seas, stars, mountains, etc.) has a voice, just as mankind does. In Revelation 5:13, the Greek word for "saying" is "legontos" and it means "to cry out" or "command". This parallels what Jesus was referring to in Luke 19:40 when He made mention of the rocks crying out if men were to be silent. Such is what is taking place with creation here in Revelation 5:13 prior to the time for all men to witness His glorious appearance.

Think about how we can be emotionally affected by creation during various seasons. Look at how rainy seasons in the fall dampen many people's spirits, while the sunny days of spring bring hope and excitement, or how boisterous seas and vehement winds seem to demonstrate anger. Creation and nature constantly speak all around us. How much more are and will their voices be heard testifying, glorifying, and worshipping in the presence of Christ (the Lamb) as depicted here in Revelation 5:13.

REVELATION 6

Overview

Revelation 6 brings us to the great tribulation period leading up to the millennium lockdown of Satan, his release for a short time, and then God's final judgment (Revelation 20). In Matthew 24:8, Jesus refers to this period as "the beginning of birth pains." Much of what Jesus foretells to His disciples in Matthew 24:6-22 correlates with what is to take place in Revelation chapters 6 through 11. Here in Revelation 6, we're provided insight regarding what's being released by the breaking of the first six of seven seals of the book (which was obtained by the Lamb from the Father). The breaking of seals 1 through 4 is introduced by each of the four living creatures which were identified in Revelation chapters 4 and 5. When each seal is broken, a different horse is released with a rider fulfilling its assignment of delivering various afflictions – very similar to what Jesus reveals in Matthew 24:6-22. The first seal releases war and thirst for power; the second withholds peace and releases conflict (resulting in mankind killing one another – civil war); the third releases an imbalance of the economy; and the fourth releases widespread death over one fourth of the earth via famine, homicides, etc. The breaking of the fifth seal reveals the cry of past martyrs for vengeance as they are told to wait patiently for other martyrs to join them from the great tribulation period. The breaking of the sixth seal brings about cosmic disturbances which literally rain terror on earth. The discovery to be addressed is:

1. Who are the martyrs?

Scriptural Reading

[1]I saw that the Lamb opened one of the seven seals, and I heard one of the four living creatures saying, as with a voice of thunder, "Come and see!" [2]Then a white horse appeared, and he who sat on it had a bow. A crown was given to him, and he came out conquering, and to conquer.
[3]When he opened the second seal, I heard the second living creature saying, "Come!" [4]Another came out, a red horse. To him who sat on it was given power to take peace from the earth, and that they should kill one another. There was given to him a great sword.
[5]When he opened the third seal, I heard the third living creature saying, "Come and see!" And behold, a black horse, and he who sat on it had a balance in his hand. [6]I heard a voice in the middle of the four living creatures saying, "A choenix of wheat for a denarius, and three choenix of barley for a denarius! Don't damage the oil and the wine!"
[7]When he opened the fourth seal, I heard the fourth living creature saying, "Come and see!" [8]And behold, a pale horse, and the name of he who sat on it was Death. Hades followed with him. Authority over one fourth of the earth, to kill with the sword, with famine, with death, and by the wild animals of the earth was given to him.
[9]When he opened the fifth seal, I saw underneath the altar the souls of those who had been killed for the Word of God, and for the testimony of the Lamb which they had. [10]They cried with a loud voice, saying, "How long, Master, the holy and true, until you judge and avenge our blood on those who dwell on the earth?" [11]A long white robe was given to each of them. They were told that they should rest yet for a while, until their fellow

servants and their brothers, who would also be killed even as they were, should complete their course. ^{12}I saw when he opened the sixth seal, and there was a great earthquake. The sun became black as sackcloth made of hair, and the whole moon became as blood. ^{13}The stars of the sky fell to the earth, like a fig tree dropping its unripe figs when it is shaken by a great wind. ^{14}The sky was removed like a scroll when it is rolled up. Every mountain and island was moved out of its place. ^{15}The kings of the earth, the princes, the commanding officers, the rich, the strong, and every slave and free person, hid themselves in the caves and in the rocks of the mountains. ^{16}They told the mountains and the rocks, "Fall on us, and hide us from the face of him who sits on the throne, and from the wrath of the Lamb, ^{17}for the great day of his wrath has come, and who is able to stand?"

Questions & Discovery

More Martyrs to Come

Who are the martyrs (Revelation 6:9-11)?

The online Oxford dictionary defines martyr as, "a person who is killed or made to suffer because of their religious or other belief." Here in Revelation 6:10, it makes very clear that those crying out for vengeance are those literally martyred because of their testimony of Jesus and upholding their belief in the Word of God. When reading this passage, what comes to mind for many of us are prominent martyrs like the Apostles and those Christians who were massacred during the reign and terror of Nero. What they have suffered very few (if any) modern-day Christians can identify with. Nowadays, most proclaimed "Christians" would have little to no evidence of being a follower of Christ if they were to be charged in a court of law. As a matter of fact, for many, if ever brought before a high court it would be for impersonating a Christian.

No need to fret, feel hopeless, or lose heart. There's another case that establishes all believers as martyrs for Christ and that is having to suffer death – it's the one curse we're all under because of our inherited sin nature (Romans 5:12). John 10:10 identifies the culprit behind death as being the thief (Satan). He (Satan) is the one who has the power of death (Hebrews 2:14), which brings an end to the state of our natural bodies and seeks to do the same with us spiritually. This group of martyrs (found within the churches mentioned in Revelation 2 and 3) consists of those who have truly surrendered their lives to Christ but are still having to contend with the sinful penalty of death. The beauty of this is knowing that Christ has defeated death and will do away with it once and for all (Revelation 20:14). As these believers' time on earth comes to an end by death, their souls join that group of martyrs mentioned in Revelation 6:10 crying out for vengeance.

Remember that Jesus came to wage war and bring division, separating what is His from what is not (Luke 12:51-53). Likewise, this is the manifestation of Christ fulfilling His proclamation by the breaking of the seven seals, releasing the full strength of attacks against what we find value, security, and peace in (i.e., rulers, economy, material things) – all for the sake of gathering His sheep to salvation from the complete wrath of God, which will result in utter destruction of death and hell in the lake of fire. For the modern-day Christians who die prior to and during these occurrences taking place in Revelation 6 and forward, they will be included with the martyrs of the past (Revelation 6:9-11). God's answer of vengeance will ultimately be doled out (on behalf of those in Christ) upon Satan and his followers, who orchestrate sin and death, which affects all of mankind (Romans 3:23 and Romans 5:12).

REVELATION 7

Overview

Continuing during the tribulation period, in this chapter John introduces us to what many consider to be the "mysterious" 144,000 and them receiving the seal of God. Midway through this chapter, he then shares the vision of witnessing a great multitude of believers proclaiming, "Salvation be to our God, who sits on the throne, and to the Lamb!" (Revelation 7:10). They're recognized as being those who have died and came out of the tribulation (from every tribe, people and language) and are now positioned before God's throne (Revelation 7:14-15). The description and purpose of the multitude of believers is discussed within this chapter. As for the 144,000 representing the tribes of Israel, there have been ongoing debates regarding their identity and purpose. Therefore, the following discoveries will be discussed and examined in greater detail:

1. Who are the 144,000?
2. What is the significance of the 144,000 receiving the seal of God?

Scriptural Reading

[1]After this, I saw four angels standing at the four corners of the earth, holding the four winds of the earth, so that no wind would blow on the earth, or on the sea, or on any tree. [2]I saw another angel ascend from the sunrise, having the seal of the living God. He cried with a loud voice to the four angels to whom it was given to harm the earth and the sea, [3]saying, "Don't harm the earth, the sea, or the trees, until we have sealed the bondservants of our God on their foreheads!" [4]I heard the number of those who were sealed, one hundred forty-four thousand, sealed out of every tribe of the children of Israel:
[5]of the tribe of Judah twelve thousand were sealed,
of the tribe of Reuben twelve thousand,
of the tribe of Gad twelve thousand,
[6]of the tribe of Asher twelve thousand,
of the tribe of Naphtali twelve thousand,
of the tribe of Manasseh twelve thousand,
[7]of the tribe of Simeon twelve thousand,
of the tribe of Levi twelve thousand,
of the tribe of Issachar twelve thousand,
[8]of the tribe of Zebulun twelve thousand,
of the tribe of Joseph twelve thousand, and
of the tribe of Benjamin twelve thousand were sealed.
[9]After these things I looked, and behold, a great multitude which no man could count, out of every nation and of all tribes, peoples, and languages, standing before the throne and before the Lamb, dressed in white robes, with palm branches in their hands. [10]They cried with a loud voice, saying, "Salvation be to our God, who sits on the throne, and to the Lamb!"
[11]All the angels were standing around the throne, the elders, and the four living creatures; and they fell on their faces before his throne, and worshiped God, [12]saying, "Amen! Blessing, glory, wisdom, thanksgiving, honor, power, and might, be to our God forever and ever! Amen."
[13]One of the elders answered, saying to me, "These who are arrayed in the white robes, who are they, and where did they come from?"

¹⁴I told him, "My lord, you know." He said to me, "These are those who came out of the great suffering. They washed their robes and made them white in the Lamb's blood. ¹⁵Therefore they are before the throne of God, and they serve him day and night in his temple. He who sits on the throne will spread his tabernacle over them. ¹⁶They will never be hungry or thirsty anymore. The sun won't beat on them, nor any heat; ¹⁷for the Lamb who is in the middle of the throne shepherds them and leads them to springs of life-giving waters. And God will wipe away every tear from their eyes."

Questions & Discovery

And, You Are?

Who are the 144,000 (Revelation 7:3-8)?

The 144,000 are acknowledged as being children of Israel (Revelation 7:4-8). The word "children" in the Greek is "huiōn" and it literally means "sons" (being of male gender). As a result, they are males who were virgins, considered as a special offering (consecration) to God and to the Lamb, and found without fault (Revelation 14:4-5). By them being virgins and without fault, there's a strong possibility they were young men around the bar mitzvah age of 13. On the other hand, they could very well be a mixture of young and old men from orthodox Judaism who were committed to the laws and traditions of the Torah. In either case, they will become converted Jews who are convinced of Jesus being the Christ. With their conversion comes the favor of God bestowed upon them in the form of receiving God's seal of approval, divine protection, and acceptance into the fold as God's chosen people. Also, because they will receive God's seal during the period of tribulation, it affords them protection from His wrath upon the earth that will occur (Revelation 9:4).

They Now Know

What is the significance of the 144,000 receiving the seal of God (Revelation 7:4)?

Let's have a brief moment of history, which in turn will bring us to the significance of the 144,000 receiving the seal of God. Ever since Jesus arrived on the scene, Jews following orthodox Judaism have struggled tremendously in accepting the notion of Jesus as the Messiah (John 10:22-42). He didn't fit into their vision of what a king would be and as a savior of the Jewish people. He walked among sinners, called the Jewish leaders out for their hypocrisy, and resisted an outright haughty promotion of Himself as the Christ. All of this led to prominent Jewish leaders rejecting Him, His teachings, and His disciples and their teachings about Him. By them rejecting Him, they were rejecting the way to God through Him (Romans 10:1-4). In doing so, they became broken branches from the olive tree (which symbolizes Israel as the chosen people of God) and opened the door for the Gentiles (non-Jews) to be grafted in because of their believing and accepting of Jesus as the Christ (Romans 11:17-24). Here's the kicker: God not only permitted, but orchestrated a portion of the Jews to reject Jesus, in order for the message of Jesus to be taken to the rest of the world for the sake of extending salvation to all (Romans 11:25).

This brings us to the introduction of the 144,000 in Revelation 7. Romans 11:26 proclaims that once the fullness of the Gentiles has come to God, He [God] will release the stubbornness of the Jews' hearts so that they, too, can see and accept Jesus as the Christ and be grafted in again. It is during the tribulation period when the fullness of Gentiles is completed and received. Afterward, the 144,000 will receive God's seal of approval, completeness and protection as they return to the fold as firstfruits unto God, brought on by His mercy (Romans 11:28-32). They needed to have God's seal in order to not be affected by the wrath of God, which was being poured out on earth during the time of tribulation that takes place upon the breaking of the seventh seal (Revelation 7:3 and 9:4).

Not only were they needing to have God's seal upon them for protection against His wrath during the tribulation period, it also solidified Israel being God's chosen people in accordance with

Deuteronomy 14:2. Due to God's seal upon them, they were redeemed by God from the earth and from among the people of the earth as He received them as consecrated unto Himself – securing Israel's position as His chosen people (Revelation 14:1-5). At some point during the tribulation period (between Revelation 8 – 14), those having God's seal upon them were either killed or raptured (unknown for certain) as John sees them united with the Lamb on Mount Zion, singing a new song with lyrics known by them only (Revelation 14:1-3).

Interestingly and biblically, the number 12,000 represents completeness, perfection and divine protection – uniquely comparable to what God considers acceptable as firstfruits consecrated to Him (Exodus 13:2, 14 and 15). Consequently, the number 144,000 represents the full satisfaction of Israel's redemption through their belief in Christ and being grafted in again (Romans 11:23-32) - a consecration of 12,000 from each of the 12 tribes of Israel (God's chosen people).

REVELATION 8

Overview

Delving into this chapter, we're reconnected for the seventh and final seal to be broken. The breaking of the seventh seal introduces seven angels standing before God and each provided with a trumpet. Prior to the trumpets sounding, another angel proceeds to add incense to the prayers of all the saints on the golden altar as the smoke is sent up before God. As the breaking of the seven seals comes to an end, the second wave of God's judgment is poured out, brought on by the sounding of each of the seven trumpets. Each wave of God's judgment (i.e., seven seals, seven trumpets, and seven bowls) is progressively worse than the last and serves as His judgment on sin. Also, each serves as an outcry of His mercy extended to the lost, all the while ushering in the second coming of Jesus. Here in Revelation 8, the first four trumpets being sounded causes chaos among the vegetation, seas, river and spring waters, and the heavens. Afterward, John sees an eagle flying in mid heaven shouting the warnings, "Woe! Woe! Woe!" because of the final three trumpets to be sounded, which will dreadfully affect mankind. The following discovery will be discussed and examined:

1. What is the significance of the angel offering to God the smoke of incense mingled with the prayers of the saints from the golden altar?

Scriptural Reading

[1]When he opened the seventh seal, there was silence in heaven for about half an hour. [2]I saw the seven angels who stand before God, and seven trumpets were given to them.

[3]Another angel came and stood over the altar, having a golden censer. Much incense was given to him, that he should add it to the prayers of all the saints on the golden altar which was before the throne. [4]The smoke of the incense, with the prayers of the saints, went up before God out of the angel's hand. [5]The angel took the censer, and he filled it with the fire of the altar, then threw it on the earth. Thunders, sounds, lightnings, and an earthquake followed.

[6]The seven angels who had the seven trumpets prepared themselves to sound.

[7]The first sounded, and there followed hail and fire, mixed with blood, and they were thrown to the earth. One third of the earth was burned up, and one third of the trees were burned up, and all green grass was burned up.

[8]The second angel sounded, and something like a great burning mountain was thrown into the sea. One third of the sea became blood, [9]and one third of the living creatures which were in the sea died. One third of the ships were destroyed.

[10]The third angel sounded, and a great star fell from the sky, burning like a torch, and it fell on one third of the rivers, and on the springs of water. [11]The name of the star is "Wormwood." One third of the waters became wormwood. Many people died from the waters, because they were made bitter.

[12]The fourth angel sounded, and one third of the sun was struck, and one third of the moon, and one third of the stars, so that one third of them would be darkened; and the day wouldn't shine for one third of it, and the night in the same way. [13]I saw, and I heard an eagle, flying in mid heaven, saying with a loud voice,

"Woe! Woe! Woe to those who dwell on the earth, because of the other blasts of the trumpets of the three angels, who are yet to sound!"

Questions & Discovery

The Ascension

What is the significance of the angel offering to God the smoke of incense mingled with the prayers of the saints from the golden altar (Revelation 8:3-5)?

In Exodus 30:7-9, Moses received specific instructions from God to pass onto Aaron (the appointed Levitical priest) the task of burning sweet-smelling incense on the altar (stationed near the curtain by the ark of the testimony, where God met with Moses) in the morning and evening of every day unto God. The sweet-smelling incense was specifically made as a consecration to God and was forbidden from being duplicated for any other use (Exodus 30:34-38). Neither was the altar to be used for burning any other strange/profane incense nor for burnt sacrifices, meat offerings, or drink offerings. What this metaphorically represented was a show of holiness and honor to God, as well as His acceptability of the people. Although this occurred in the Old Testament and was a procedural function of the Levitical priests, the same principle applies today in how we're to meet with God in a way which reverences and honors Him as holy and above anyone and/or anything, and we're to be found acceptable to Him (which in Christ, we are).

In Exodus, we read that the altar was set up for God to meet with Moses or whichever appointed spiritual leader afterward. Today, it is because of Jesus that each of us is able to meet with Him (2 Corinthians 5:18). However, we must be mindful of this statement made by Jesus in John 4:24, "God is spirit, and those who worship him must worship in spirit and truth." What this translates to is our prayers to the Father being delivered by Jesus, who is our advocate (1 John 2:1), meaning he intercedes on our behalf (Romans 8:34).

Please be sure to take your time reading and grasping the following information.

In John 4:24, it is affirmed that God is spirit. The word "spirit" is translated from the Greek word "pneuma", which means "breath" – symbolizing that which is unseen (but it exists, much like the wind). Unlike whatever is in the atmosphere affecting the wind (changing its odor, direction, speed, etc.), God (being spirit) is holy, pure, and divine – incapable of being contaminated or changed by anyone or anything (Malachi 3:6). So, for mankind to worship Him in spirit and truth, we must and can only do so by having Jesus as our advocate when we pray to God. Jesus represents the incense (acceptable sacrifice) on the altar as well as the smoke (spirit) of the incense from the altar which goes to the Father (Hebrews 9:14). Picture that every time we pray to God, it is Jesus (the burning incense) on the altar interceding on our behalf by presenting/relaying our petitions (in spirit (depicted as smoke)) to the Father and advocating for whatever our needs are (1 John 5:14-15).

This brings us to answering the lead question, "What is the significance of the angel offering the smoke of incense mingled with the prayers of the saints from the golden altar to God?" By sin bringing death upon all mankind, when believers experience death and because of death, it (death) must be met with retribution for its trespassing offense against those in Christ, belonging to God. See, not only did Jesus pay the wages (death) for our sins, which places us in right standing with God (Romans 6:23 and 2 Corinthians 5:18-21), but by His resurrection He also seized authority over death and hell (Revelation 1:18). So, although when we die, we are secured with and in Christ, figuratively our voices (i.e., prayers, cries) become part of a "class action lawsuit" demanding justice against death – just as Abel's blood cried out when he was slain by Cain (Genesis 4:10).

The metaphorical depiction John observes are the believers' prayers, pleas, and cries for justice, which are positioned under the altar (Revelation 6:9-10). The prayers for justice (by the believers) represent what kindles the fire underneath the altar and flames the acceptable incense (Jesus) to the point of releasing the smoke (Him advocating) to the Father on their behalf. See, the prayers of believers can never nor will ever be answered without Jesus' intervening – He is the only way we can worship God in spirit and truth (John 14:6). Now, although Jesus advocates before the Father on behalf of the believers, the answer(s) will be provided according to God's will and timing (Ecclesiastes 3:1-8). However, believers can rest assured that He will execute vengeance on their behalf (Romans 12:19). Here in Revelation 8:3-5, God's will and timing for answering the saints' prayers for justice is portrayed by the angel dishing out and throwing fire from the altar to the earth – releasing and starting the second phase of God's wrath via the seven trumpets.

REVELATION 9

Overview

Here in Revelation 9, the sounding of the trumpets resume with introductions of the first woe (5th trumpet) and the second woe (6th trumpet). The word "woe" comes from the Greek word "ouai" and is used to express deep distress, lamentation, or denunciation. They (the "woes") are permitted by God and executed at the hand of the fallen angels (Revelation 9:1, 14, and 15). Each of the three woes (Revelation 9 through 19) represent gradual levels of God's judgements against mankind (unbelievers), those who reject Him in favor of their own lusts, pride, ideologies, gods, disbeliefs, etc. The "woes" do not serve as an appeasement to God but rather as an appeal by God for them to repent. However, just like with Pharaoh and his army, as the damage of each woe desisted, they resented God more and their hearts were hardened (Exodus 8:15 and Revelation 9:20 and 21). The first woe brought on severe suffering (pain and agony) to non-believers for a period of six months, whereas the second woe was permitted to kill a third of mankind with fire, smoke and sulfur.

Revelation 9:4 supports the idea of believers being alive and having to endure/overcome during this time of God's judgement. For certain, we know that those among the believers are the appointed 144,000 identified in Revelation 7 and Revelation 14:1-5. What many question is whether there will be other believers from the Gentiles around during this period. As examined and explained in Revelation 7 of this book, Gentile believers will be around and are encouraged to endure/overcome with the specific instructions provided to each church (see Revelation 2 and 3 regarding those of the churches of Sardis, Pergamum, Ephesus, Thyatira, Smyrna, and Laodicea). The following discoveries will be discussed and examined:

1. What is the significance of the fallen "star" receiving a key?
2. What is the abyss?
3. What does the great river Euphrates represent in Revelation 9:14?
4. What does fire, smoke, and sulfur actually represent?

Scriptural Reading

[1]The fifth angel sounded, and I saw a star from the sky which had fallen to the earth. The key to the pit of the abyss was given to him. [2]He opened the pit of the abyss, and smoke went up out of the pit, like the smoke from a burning furnace. The sun and the air were darkened because of the smoke from the pit. [3]Then out of the smoke came locusts on the earth, and power was given to them, as the scorpions of the earth have power. [4]They were told that they should not hurt the grass of the earth, neither any green thing, neither any tree, but only those people who don't have God's seal on their foreheads. [5]They were given power, not to kill them, but to torment them for five months. Their torment was like the torment of a scorpion when it strikes a person. [6]In those days people will seek death, and will in no way find it. They will desire to die, and death will flee from them.
[7]The shapes of the locusts were like horses prepared for war. On their heads were something like golden crowns, and their faces were like people's faces. [8]They had hair like women's hair, and their teeth were like those of lions. [9]They had breastplates like breastplates of iron. The sound of their wings

was like the sound of many chariots and horses rushing to war. [10]They have tails like those of scorpions, with stingers. In their tails they have power to harm men for five months. [11]They have over them as king the angel of the abyss. His name in Hebrew is "Abaddon", but in Greek, he has the name "Apollyon". [12]The first woe is past. Behold, there are still two woes coming after this.

[13]The sixth angel sounded. I heard a voice from the horns of the golden altar which is before God, [14]saying to the sixth angel who had the trumpet, "Free the four angels who are bound at the great river Euphrates!"

[15]The four angels were freed who had been prepared for that hour and day and month and year, so that they might kill one third of mankind. [16]The number of the armies of the horsemen was two hundred million. I heard the number of them. [17]Thus I saw the horses in the vision and those who sat on them, having breastplates of fiery red, hyacinth blue, and sulfur yellow; and the horses' heads resembled lions' heads. Out of their mouths proceed fire, smoke, and sulfur. [18]By these three plagues, one third of mankind was killed: by the fire, the smoke, and the sulfur, which proceeded out of their mouths. [19]For the power of the horses is in their mouths and in their tails. For their tails are like serpents, and have heads; and with them they harm.

[20]The rest of mankind, who were not killed with these plagues, didn't repent of the works of their hands, that they wouldn't worship demons, and the idols of gold, and of silver, and of brass, and of stone, and of wood, which can't see, hear, or walk. [21]They didn't repent of their murders, their sorceries, their sexual immorality, or their thefts.

Questions & Discovery

The Key

What is the significance of the fallen "star" receiving a key (Revelation 9:1)?

The first question one may ask is, "Who or what is this fallen 'star'?" In order to answer that question, a brief background is needed for proper comprehension. Biblically, when the word "star" is used as either a proper noun or proper pronoun it signifies a person or entity (i.e., a celestial being) within the heavenly realm. In Revelation 12:4 and 7-9, it shares how Satan and a third of the "stars" (referring to angels) were cast out of heaven; Revelation 22:16 describes Jesus as the Bright and Morning Star; and, Isaiah 14:12 refers to Lucifer (proper name of Satan) as "the morning star" as translated from the Hebrew word "hê·lêl". With that being said, it would be correct to suppose the fallen "star" in Revelation 9:1 is none other than one of the fallen angels which followed in the ways of Satan. Another eye-opener worth noting is where many of the fallen angels currently reside. According to Ephesians 6:12, they along with Satan exist in the heavenly realm (below God's space). They not only operate in that realm, but also within the jurisdiction of this world, according to Ephesians 2:1-2. This explains why John was able to witness a "star" falling to the earth from the sky when the fifth angel sounded the fifth trumpet.

To answer the lead question, now that it is clear who/what the fallen "star" is, let's delve into the significance of the "key" as mentioned in Revelation 9:1. The word "key" derives from the Greek word "kleis" which means to "shut" or "close", with a literal and figurative reference to the authority to lock or unlock. The "key" which the fallen star receives is the authority to loosen what has been bound in the abyss. This authority was granted by God specifically for the purpose of judgment during this first "woe" period. As annotated in Matthew 28:18 and Revelation 1:18, we find that Jesus has all authority and dominion, as well as holds the keys to death and hades. We know from Job 1and 1 Peter 5:8, that Satan has boundaries and must obtain permission from God (with God always having a greater purpose) to attack His children. Here in Revelation 9, God does not allow the locusts to harm any of those who have His seal upon them; however, He yet shows mercy to the unbelievers by limiting the amount of harm imposed upon them to five months (without causing death) for the sake of them coming to repentance.

In a nutshell, the significance of the fallen "star" receiving a key (authority) was solely for the purpose of fulfilling God's will.

The Abyss

What is the abyss (Revelation 9:1-2)?

The word "abyss" comes from the Greek word "abyssou" which means "bottomless". Scripturally, it is oftentimes referred to as a complete darkened place created for Satan and his followers (2 Peter 2:4 and Revelation 20:1). According to Matthew 8:12, it is also to be a place for non-believers and rejectors of Jesus. Probably the most relatable description of the abyss would be what we know as the astronomical object called the black hole (located in outer space). Just like the abyss, whatever enters the black hole can in no way escape.

Something else to be learned here in Revelation 9:1-2 is that within the abyss there appears to be a pit. This word "pit" originates from the Greek word "phreatos", meaning "well" or "shaft". Much like a prison has a special place for hardened criminals, the same can be said for the abyss having solitary confinement accommodations for demonic beings, possibly separating them from mankind non-believers and rejectors of Christ who are sentenced to eternal separation and darkness (Matthew 8:12 and 2 Thessalonians 1:9). These demonic beings' sole purpose is for tormenting and destroying, which may be a reason the king angel over them is called "Abaddon" in Hebrew and "Apollyon" in Greek, signifying "destruction" and "Destroyer" respectively (Revelation 9:11).

The Great River Euphrates

What does the great river Euphrates represent in Revelation 9:14?

Throughout the Bible, water is literally and figuratively used in describing the word of God in various natures and instances. We can find it being used symbolically in baptisms (Hebrews 10:22); for cleansing, as in "husbands washing their wives as Christ washes the church" (Ephesians 5:26); and as living water offered to the Samaritan woman at the well. Here in Revelation 9:14, the great river Euphrates figuratively serves another purpose of God's word – it represents His great mercy, which simultaneously acts as a standard/barrier between either receiving compassion or receiving chastisement. God, being Wisdom (Proverbs 8), chooses when to justly demonstrate either as He sees fit for a greater purpose.

The significance of the great river Euphrates representing the word of God is that it illustrates God lifting up a standard against the enemy (Isaiah 59:19), which limits the timing and boundaries of the enemy. We know from John 1:1-2 that Jesus is the Word of God, and Jesus possesses all authority (Matthew 28:18). It is this great river Euphrates (Word of God) which holds back the four angels who will kill a third of mankind at an appointed time (Revelation 9:15), rendering partial justice on behalf of His children while extending mercy for the remaining two thirds to repent (which they refuse to do).

Fire, Smoke, and Sulfur

What does fire, smoke, and sulfur actually represent (Revelation 9:17-18)?

In verses 13-21 of Revelation 6, we're introduced to the sixth trumpet being sounded and a second event (within the second "woe") taking place. It is a release of four angels freed to kill one third of mankind by plagues. The weaponized plagues used to accomplish this severe feat are identified as fire, smoke, and sulfur (Revelation 9:18). It beckons two questions. First, is this vision presenting a metaphorical or literal account? Second, if metaphorical, how so? Let's tackle the first question to decipher whether this vision is metaphorical or literal. In verses 14 and 15, we find there are four angels released and given the mission of killing one third of mankind who are present on earth during this period. However, in verse 16, we read that accompanying these four angels to carry out this major operation are armies consisting of 200,000,000 horsemen. What's even more mind-boggling is how the mission of killing one third of mankind was carried out by these 200,000,000 horsemen.

One would think weaponry such as firearms, knives, or some more modernized weapons would be used. But neither of those were utilized in John's vision. Instead, in verses 18 and 19, we find that it was what came forth out of their horses mouths that killed one third of mankind. What came forth out of their mouths were fire, smoke, and sulfur (i.e., brimstone). So, are we to instinctively assume that 200,000,000 horsemen traveled throughout the entire world riding horses which spewed fire, smoke, and sulfur from their mouths at random individuals, killing one third of them? With God, we know that this could very well be literally plausible, for Jesus declares in Luke 1:37, "…for with God all things are possible." However, during these periods of "woes", God isn't seeking to destroy mankind but to bring them to a state of repentance. What these "woes" are unleashing are consequences for sin which God has been withholding (by His mercy). Mankind, by continually rejecting God and believing within themselves to have no need of Him, in essence is asking for His mercy and protection to be removed from them as well. Because He's longsuffering (2 Peter 3:9), He allows for them to experience life with limited consequences without Him. As previously stated, each "woe" brings gradual dire consequences. These consequences are commensurate with the sins that have been committed. The sins they are being judged for are identified in verses 20 and 21. Although John paints for us a vivid picture of what is to take place, there's a foretelling message within the vision. So, the answer to the first question is that this vision of John's is metaphorical.

Now that it has been identified as metaphorical, let's decipher what this fire, smoke and sulfur (brimstone) are that will kill one third of mankind. Seeing that consequences are commensurate with the sins committed, the four released angels will put into action their well-orchestrated strategy by using demonic spiritual armies to heavily influence mankind (killing a third and harming many others (verses 18-19)) within a short span of time (verse 15). This indeed will be done by what the three plagues represent (or what mankind refused to repent of in verses 19-20) as lovers of themselves (2 Timothy 3:2):

- Fire: being totally engulfed in immorality (Romans 1:26-32)
- Smoke: walking blindly (Zephaniah 1:17 and Matthew 15:14)
- Sulfur (brimstone): displaying destructive behavior (Genesis 6:11)

The selfish and sinful passions of mankind will be unlimitedly fed and reinforced by demonic spirits, resulting in major occurrences of suicides, homicides, and genocides. Remember in verse 17 where it stated the horses' heads were like heads of lions? Lions represent courage and horses represent speed. These demonic spirits will give mankind the courage to speedily self-destruct. Sadly, the other two thirds of mankind will continue in their ways without repenting.

REVELATION 10

Overview

Continuing with the events of the second "woe", in this chapter John provides for us a symbolic dramatic picture of a mighty angel coming from heaven. This strong angel arrives in a cloud with a rainbow over his head, a sun-radiant face, and feet like pillars of fire. He arrives with a little open book in his right hand with his right foot on the sea and his left foot on the land as he proceeds with a loud cry (as a lion's roar). He then proceeds to lift his right hand with a pledge to God of there no longer being a delay for the completed mystery of God as declared to God's prophets. Suddenly, John hears a voice from heaven instructing him to retrieve the book from the right hand of the mighty angel and eat it. He is then told to prophesy again over those who are yet alive on earth. The following discoveries will be discussed and examined:

1. What is the significance of the mighty angel arriving on the scene?
2. Why does the mighty angel pledge to God with the open book in his right hand?
3. What is the purpose of John having to prophesy to the people?

Scriptural Reading

[1]I saw a mighty angel coming down out of the sky, clothed with a cloud. A rainbow was on his head. His face was like the sun, and his feet like pillars of fire. [2]He had in his hand a little open book. He set his right foot on the sea, and his left on the land. [3]He cried with a loud voice, as a lion roars. When he cried, the seven thunders uttered their voices. [4]When the seven thunders sounded, I was about to write; but I heard a voice from the sky saying, "Seal up the things which the seven thunders said, and don't write them."

[5]The angel whom I saw standing on the sea and on the land lifted up his right hand to the sky [6]and swore by him who lives forever and ever, who created heaven and the things that are in it, the earth and the things that are in it, and the sea and the things that are in it, that there will no longer be delay, [7]but in the days of the voice of the seventh angel, when he is about to sound, then the mystery of God is finished, as he declared to his servants the prophets.

[8]The voice which I heard from heaven, again speaking with me, said, "Go, take the book which is open in the hand of the angel who stands on the sea and on the land."

[9]I went to the angel, telling him to give me the little book. He said to me, "Take it and eat it. It will make your stomach bitter, but in your mouth it will be as sweet as honey."

[10]I took the little book out of the angel's hand and ate it. It was as sweet as honey in my mouth. When I had eaten it, my stomach was made bitter. [11]They told me, "You must prophesy again over many peoples, nations, languages, and kings."

Questions & Discovery

The Mighty Angel

What is the significance of the mighty angel arriving on the scene (Revelation 10:1-4)?

The significance of the mighty angel's arrival lies within his appearance, his possession, his stance, and his cry. Let's examine each. According to John's observation, his appearance consisted of being wrapped in a cloud, a rainbow over his head, a sun-radiant face, and feet (or legs) of fire. Being wrapped in a cloud represents the coming presence and glory of God as a Christophany (i.e., appearance or non-physical manifestation of Christ) just as He was presented in Exodus 13:21 and Exodus 19:9. The rainbow over his head serves as a reminder of His covenant made with Noah, all mankind, and all living creatures that have life (Genesis 9:1-17). Part of that covenant includes not only God not ever destroying every living creature with water again, but also God instituting capital punishment (Genesis 9:6) – holding everyone accountable for his or her offenses. His shining face depicts his blessing of favor and mercy shown toward mankind (Numbers 6:24-26). And his feet (or legs) of fire signify a time for purifying (Numbers 31:23).

In this mighty angel's possession was a little open book. Without a doubt, this book exemplifies the law of Moses (commonly referred to as the Torah – the first five books of the Bible) which is the foundational basis of moral law. It is by this book that Christ has authority to execute judgement (Matthew 5:17). The stance of Him having one foot in the sea and one on the land is a proclamation of all living creatures being accountable to Him and being under His authority (Matthew 28:18). Finally, his cry as a lion's roar delivers a fair warning that believers can be comforted by (knowing it is nearing the time of the return of Christ), but non-believers should be (but aren't) very fearful of. Overall, this metaphorical event displays the totality of God's coming judgement in righteousness, without reservation nor being unjustly executed.

The Pledge

Why does the mighty angel pledge to God with the open book in his right hand (Revelation 10:5-7)?

Having his right hand lifted (while holding the open book in it) and vowing to God serves as a testament of truth and justification as to what is about to occur (in the form of judgement) and why. This vow couldn't be made by man nor angel to God, but by God Himself to Himself, since there is none greater to overturn the sentence nor enforce the vow (Hebrews 6:13). As litigant, the mighty angel presenting the facts within the open book was sufficient evidence for God to impose righteous judgment.

This is Coming

What is the purpose of John having to prophesy to the people (Revelation 10:8-11)?

John was told to take the book from the mighty angel and eat it. A figurative tale, it's meaning is literally bittersweet. Although it would taste sweet in his mouth, it would make his stomach sour. As previously stated, the book represented the law, and according to Psalm 19:7, "The Law of the Lord is perfect…" Knowing that Jesus is the fulfillment of the Law and the Prophets, this made the taste sweet (i.e., acceptably pleasant) for John. However, as it entered His stomach, the bitterness sets in, which represents the reality of what is to occur as judgement.

After figuratively eating the book, John was told that he must again prophesy to "peoples, nations, languages, and kings." The reason John was having to prophesy to the people is because what he had eaten (the book) wasn't for him to keep to himself, but to regurgitate God's forthcoming verdict upon the peoples, nations, languages, and kings. The purpose for John prophesying to those beings is to warn, with hopes of them repenting to avoid eternal punishment.

Just like John, we as believers today are not to savior the taste of Christ in our mouths as a sweet satisfaction for ourselves. We must digest His word and allow it to permeate our insides. As it works its way inside of us and through us, it performs a bitter transformation of us, stripping us of what we're comfortable with and who we're comfortable being (in the flesh). It affects us with compassion to the point of it needing to be regurgitated in our speech and actions, promoting Christ to others for the sake of their souls.

REVELATION 11

Overview

In this chapter, John is provided specific instructions about "measuring" God's property as he prepares to observe a series of metaphorical events to take place leading to the fullness of God's judgement. We find there's an introduction of two persons (possessing specific powers) coming on the scene as God's witnesses, who are killed and resurrected (bringing an end to the second woe). Lastly, we are provided insight to the beginnings of the last "woe" as the seventh angel sounds the seventh trumpet. The following discoveries will be discussed and examined:

1. What is the significant meaning behind Revelation 11:1-6?
2. What is the significance of the two witnesses being killed?
3. What is the significance of the two witnesses being resurrected?
4. What is the significance of the seventh angel sounding the seventh trumpet?

Scriptural Reading

¹A reed like a rod was given to me. Someone said, "Rise and measure God's temple, and the altar, and those who worship in it. ²Leave out the court which is outside of the temple, and don't measure it, for it has been given to the nations. They will tread the holy city under foot for forty-two months. ³I will give power to my two witnesses, and they will prophesy one thousand two hundred sixty days, clothed in sackcloth."

⁴These are the two olive trees and the two lamp stands, standing before the Lord of the earth. ⁵If anyone desires to harm them, fire proceeds out of their mouth and devours their enemies. If anyone desires to harm them, he must be killed in this way. ⁶These have the power to shut up the sky, that it may not rain during the days of their prophecy. They have power over the waters, to turn them into blood, and to strike the earth with every plague, as often as they desire.

⁷When they have finished their testimony, the beast that comes up out of the abyss will make war with them, and overcome them, and kill them. ⁸Their dead bodies will be in the street of the great city, which spiritually is called Sodom and Egypt, where also their Lord was crucified. ⁹From among the peoples, tribes, languages, and nations, people will look at their dead bodies for three and a half days, and will not allow their dead bodies to be laid in a tomb. ¹⁰Those who dwell on the earth will rejoice over them, and they will be glad. They will give gifts to one another, because these two prophets tormented those who dwell on the earth.

¹¹After the three and a half days, the breath of life from God entered into them, and they stood on their feet. Great fear fell on those who saw them. ¹²I heard a loud voice from heaven saying to them, "Come up here!" They went up into heaven in a cloud, and their enemies saw them. ¹³In that day there was a great earthquake, and a tenth of the city fell. Seven thousand people were killed in the earthquake, and the rest were terrified and gave glory to the God of heaven.

¹⁴The second woe is past. Behold, the third woe comes quickly. ¹⁵The seventh angel sounded, and great voices in heaven followed, saying, "The kingdom of the world has become the

Kingdom of our Lord and of his Christ. He will reign forever and ever!"
[16]The twenty-four elders, who sit on their thrones before God's throne, fell on their faces and worshiped God, [17]saying: "We give you thanks, Lord God, the Almighty, the one who is and who was, because you have taken your great power and reigned. [18]The nations were angry, and your wrath came, as did the time for the dead to be judged, and to give your bondservants the prophets, their reward, as well as to the saints and those who fear your name, to the small and the great, and to destroy those who destroy the earth."
[19]God's temple that is in heaven was opened, and the ark of the Lord's covenant was seen in his temple. Lightnings, sounds, thunders, an earthquake, and great hail followed.

Questions & Discovery

What's Going On?

What is the significant meaning behind Revelation 11:1-6?

Some of what takes place in this chapter is entwined with what is to be played out in the following chapters of Revelation (12-19). In the opening, John is provided a measuring tool to separate God's property. This measuring tool is described as a "reed" (Revelation 11:1). The word "reed" comes from the Greek word "kalamos" which metaphorically describes a writing pen. Thus, leading to the instruction given to John to literally take note of what is God's property which is sealed and protected apart from what is not. He is then told that the "holy city" will be tread underfoot for forty-two months. The "holy city", as many are aware, relates to Jerusalem which means "foundation of peace" in the Greek. The abhorrent act of it being trampled underfoot denotes the demonic charged blatant disregard and blasphemies against God and the things of God by those outside the seal and protection of God (Daniel 7:8, 11, 20 and 11:36). According to Revelation 13:5, this will be allowed to take place for a period of forty-two months.

It is during this forty-two-month period, that God will bring on the scene and empower two witnesses to prophesy among those on the outside (Revelation 11:3). There are some who suggest that the two witnesses are Moses and Elijah, primarily based on what took place during Jesus' transfiguration in Matthew 17. However, we must understand that Moses had already experienced death upon fulfilling his purpose (Deuteronomy 34). So, why would God allow for him to experience death again with another purpose? It is highly unlikely. With that being the case, this would bring the most logical two witnesses to be none other than the two persons who have never experienced death because they were taken by God, for such a time as this. Those two people are Enoch and Elijah (Genesis 5:24 and 2 Kings 2:11). In Revelation 11:4, they are described as being the two olive trees and two lampstands, being interpreted as the anointed ones, and the church is providing light for repentance during those reprehensible and dire days of judgement to come. For anyone wishing to harm the two witnesses, they (two witnesses) were endowed with power to devour them with fire proceeding from their mouths. The word "harm" is translated from the Greek word "adikēsai" which implies to wickedly or unjustly accuse. The fire proceeding from the witnesses' mouths denotes the word of God effectively cutting through their false claims with truth (Jeremiah 5:14 and Hosea 6:5), therefore declaring the accusers as foolish false witnesses. Another power in the witness' possession is God's authority for retribution (Revelation 11:6), but notice that they never use this power because they understand that vengeance is God's alone (Deuteronomy 32:35).

Done for Now

What is the significance of the two witnesses being killed (Revelation 11:7-10)?

The purpose of the witnesses was not only to prophesy of what is to come (Revelation 11:3) but to suffer death and be resurrected as a demonstration of God's power and an extension of His mercy and grace reaching out to the lost. The prophetic messages offered an avenue for repentance and salvation for the lost but served as a harsh (yet truthful) judgement against Satan and those who follow after his lies and ways. This infuriated the enemy's camp to the point of them exacting capital punishment upon the witnesses as a mockery against God and a show of unity and strength among themselves. Their bodies being left in the street of the "great city" (which spiritually is called Sodom and Gomorrah) signifies being left defeated in the world, by the world, and for the world's pleasure – just as Jesus suffered public humiliation (Hebrew 13:12). It further reads that their bodies were left in the open for three and a half days and no one was allowed to properly bury them (Revelation 11:9). With this taking place outside the presence of the sealed and protected people of God, it was allowed to be so as a testament against the ungodly, signifying there was no one left (possessing courage and compassion) to bury the dead (Psalms 79:3). As a matter of fact, quite the opposite happens as they will begin to celebrate and exchange gifts as appreciation for a job well done in killing the prophets (Revelation 11:10).

They're Back

What is the significance of the two witnesses being resurrected (Revelation 11:11-14)?

Miraculously, as the two prophets are dead and laying openly in the streets, after three and a half days, God resurrects, calls, and receives them into heaven in the presence of their enemies. The prophets' purpose becomes complete as they return to their final resting place (Isaiah 60:8). Just like what occurred when Jesus died on the cross, the same occurs with the prophets going to heaven and a great earthquake happening. Ironically, the earthquake which occurred during Jesus' death brought about bodies of saints being raised from the grave (Matthew 27:52-53), whereas seven thousand will be killed during the earthquake following the prophets' resurrection (Revelation 11:13); however, both situations yield those observing being in fear and giving glory to God (Matthew 27:52-54 and Revelation 11:13). The significance of the two witnesses being resurrected points to God being the One True and Living God who possesses all power which no enemy can match (Genesis 17:1). What the enemy calls dead or intends for harm, God uses it for good and a greater purpose in His timing (Genesis 50:20 and Esther 4:14). This action brings about the end of the second "woe" (Revelation 11:14) and ushers in the third "woe" with quickness.

The Last Note

What is the significance of the seventh angel sounding the seventh trumpet (Revelation 11:15-19)?

Here at the sounding of the seventh trumpet by the seventh angel, we come to the beginning of the end which brings about the heavenly voices rejoicing at the coming of Jesus to inherit the kingdom of the world. Although Jesus' return occurs soon (in the not-so-distant future), the rejoicing takes place based on the knowledge of the end result, which is signified by the sounding of the seventh trumpet (Revelation 10:7 and Daniel 2:44). That one trumpet sound sets off an array of worship by heavenly voices and the twenty-four elders proclaiming Jesus' authority that is confirmed by Him taking great power and reigning (Revelation 1:8 and 11:17). There is also rejoicing for the judgment to take place on behalf of the saints (Revelation 12 - 19), the final destruction of Satan and his followers (Revelation 20:7-15), and the distribution of rewards to the saints (Revelation 22:12). That trumpet sound represents a time for the temple of God to be opened for all believers to bask in His presence with full satisfaction of long life (Revelation 11:19) and the rendering of judgement being accomplished. The significance of the seventh angel sounding the seventh trumpet solidifies the believers' confidence and seal of salvation in Christ from the judgment upon the world to come.

IN CLOSING

This book was written with the intent of providing insights regarding key biblical passages found within Genesis (chapters 1 through 11) and Revelation (chapters 1 through 11). The more time we spend in relationship with God and learning of Him, the more He's able to make plain what many consider the mysteries of His word. May the insights of this book stimulate within you an appetite for seeking a growing relationship with God and prepare you for what is to come.

For those who have never surrendered and made Jesus Lord and Savior of your life, or anyone having doubts about salvation, repeating this simple prayer can be the starting point in the right direction that leads to surety of eternal life with God:

> Lord, I accept the truth of you taking my sins upon the cross and dying for me. I accept the truth of you being resurrected, which gives me the opportunity for being reconciled with God. At this very critical moment, I am surrendering all that I am and have (heart, body, mind, soul, spirit, word, deed, and thoughts) unto you in exchange for having that personal relationship. I pray you have mercy on me and grant me favor and the power of your Holy Spirit to live this new life to your glory each and every day going forward. This I pray in the name of Jesus - Amen!

NOTES

1. AMG International, Inc., 1991. The Hebrew-Greek Key Study Bible (King James Version). AMG Publishers. Chattanooga, TN 37422, USA.
2. Biblical scriptures and various versions. BibleGateway. Retrieved from https://www.biblegateway.com/passage/
3. World English Bible, 1997. Holy Bible, www.eBible.org. Michael & Lori Johnson, Makawao, Hawaii 96768.

Author Owen Watson, Ph.D.

Email: drowenwatson@outlook.com

BOOKS BY
Author Owen Watson, Ph.D.

A Song in the Timing I Needed
Volume 1

It's in Their DNA: What and Why Men and Women
Do Not Ask and Do Not Answer

Relentless Grace: Behind the Scenes of Men

There is Jesus: Prayers for Life's Journey

Prayers for Life's Journey

Fighting Cancer One Poem a Day
(50 states & D.C. series)

Betting on Me: Revelatory Concepts for Success

Defeating Cancer One Poem a Day

Po' Man Ain't Got Not Much Say

What Matters Most: Family, Friends, and Foes